ROAD BLOCK TO MOSCOW

NORTH LIBERTY
MENNONITE CHURCH

ROAD BLOCK TO MOSCOW

NICK SAVOCA
with
DICK SCHNEIDER

Sketches by William Mather,
a British journalist
who accompanied the group

DIMENSION BOOKS
BETHANY FELLOWSHIP, INC.
Minneapolis, Minn. 55438

Library of Congress
Catalog Card Number 77-89445
ISBN 0-87123-489-0

This issue published in 1977 by special
arrangement with the Fleming H. Revell Company.

Names of many individuals in this book have been changed to
protect those involved.

DIMENSION BOOKS
Published by Bethany Fellowship, Inc.
6820 Auto Club Road
Minneapolis, Minnesota 55438

Printed in the United States of America

Contents

Foreword

"Unless we indulge in sanctified brutality we will never get anywhere."

Britain's political *East West Digest* quoted me as having said that in a huge rally in London where I announced this May Day Outreach.

Did I really say that?

If I did, I wish I had said it a million times more strongly. Why?

Don't ask me, I will ask *you* something.

Who is going to evangelize the Communist-controlled countries?

Who will show the world that there is no freedom of religion, of expression, of the press, and of movement?

Who is willing to put his life in the balance instead of just talking about the gospel in a safe place?

Who is going to give Bibles to the millions who have never yet seen a copy?

The answer is: only those who believe in and practise "aggressive evangelism." That means to accept Jesus' words: "*Go ye,* into *all* the world and make *all* nations my disciples." Don't wait for an invitation, don't ask permission, don't expect red-carpet treatment. Because *nobody* has the authority to invite you, nor to stop you. Jesus says: "I have been given all authority in heaven and on earth."

Therefore, go!

That's pretty strong stuff, and we are not used to it.

For hundreds of years we have had the extraordinary situation where we have seen people coming to us to get the gospel. We expected them to come and advertised our spiritual menu in the daily papers. Now we have forgotten the correct flow which God intended. It had to be through revolution, and we needed a Communist revolution to remind us of that. It had to spread through penetration, but we accepted political barriers as a convenient excuse for not having to go there.

There? It is almost half of the world.

It's militant.

It's threatening.

It's dangerous.

And the stakes are high.

The future of the whole church of Christ is at stake, and of the entire world. The above-mentioned article in *East West Digest* finished with the words: "If the church in Communist-dominated countries is to survive into the next century, it will only do so because of men like Brother Andrew."

Something will have to be done about it—something drastic.

As long as our love of money is greater than our fear of a totalitarian regime there will be no survival, much less revival. Remember that one part of the body cannot survive, be healthy, or even live, if half of it is cut off and written off.

Scores of young people decided to do something about it. They were not professionals and they probably made mistakes. They were not to take Scriptures in. "The Lord would provide." The Lord sure did. *We* took copies of the Gospels in and almost broke the hearts of the dear Russian believers when we told them that a group of young people from the West would pick the Gospels up soon and give them out on Red Square on May Day. The Russian believers pleaded with us to let them keep them, because, *"We* want to give them to people who need them."

We made a deal with them and shared the Gospels. They got the better part of it because—well, you had better read for yourself.

I saw a strange fire in the eyes of all the young people who came back from May Day. They had seen what I have seen for more than eighteen years now.

The need.

The opportunity.

And that happiness lies in obedience to the Great Commission, and not necessarily in visible results.

But there *will* be lasting results. Something has started which can never be stopped.

Who can stop it, when Jesus has said, "Go"?

BROTHER ANDREW

ROAD
BLOCK
TO
MOSCOW

1

Rendezvous in London

A London mist settled in glistening droplets on the black iron fence guarding the brooding mansion looming before me. Was this the place? I swung my heavy duffel bag from my shoulder to the damp cobblestones as I stopped to check the house number. Yes, the numbers they had given me glinted dully on the carved door of the old vicarage.

My heart caught for a moment as I stood there studying the ancient building. From it would be launched one of the most audacious adventures of its kind. And I would be part of it.

I hesitated before climbing the old stone steps. Once I touched that bell there would be no turning back. But I knew deep down that there would be no turning back for me. I had looked forward to this adventure too long. Even so, I still tingled with a strange mixture of apprehension and excitement, for I had never participated in anything even remotely like this in all of my twenty-seven years.

A strange chain of events had brought me to this foggy London street. The sequence began about three months ago when I arrived in Germany to attend a special school of Christian evangelism. It would help me, I felt, in my youth ministry back in the United States. My wife, Rozanne, and baby daughter, Anita, had accompanied me. The school promised to be a fascinating three months of study and sharing with some fifty young people from different countries about new ways to bring Christ's message to youth.

However, in the first few days of classes I began to hear three words with mysterious overtones mentioned frequently: "May Day Outreach." When Mac, an English student, referred to it during a classroom discussion, an electric current seemed to surge through the room. Later, as Mac and I walked along the parapets of the old building, I questioned him about it.

He stopped, looked at me quizzically, and said, "Do you mean that you don't know?"

"No, I'm new here, remember?"

He laughed. "I'm sorry—it's become such a subject of conversation among the kids I thought everybody was in on it." He then became very serious. "A group is going to Russia to witness for Christ."

"Not on . . . ?" I started to ask incredulously.

"Yes," he smiled, "on May Day—this coming May Day in Moscow on Red Square."

I swallowed hard. Red Square? I knew that May Day is a world holiday of communism and is especially celebrated in Russia with military parades and festivals. Moscow's Red Square is the center of it all. I recalled television news shots showing Brezhnev and other Soviet leaders reviewing troops there.

But witness in Red Square on May Day? This would be like sitting on Brezhnev's desk and trying to convert him.

"You're really asking for trouble!" I laughed. I remembered news stories about a British minister who was arrested for passing out Bibles to people in Czechoslovakia.

"Will you pass out Bibles?"

"No," said Mac, "we won't be able to bring anything like that in with us because we would be stopped right at the border. But I know something is planned; at least we will be able to talk to the people about Christ's love for them.

"What we really want to do," he emphasized, "is to call to the world's attention the Russian Christians who are suffering for Christ, and also to let these people know of our concern for them."

I knew what he meant about the suffering of Russian Christians. Despite Soviet statements of "religious freedom" and state-approved "churches," I knew that the fires of suppressed Christianity burned deep among the people. I had read reports of raids on Christian home meetings, of believers being sent off to concentration camps.

"Nick—will you come with us?"

Mac's question snapped me back to the present.

"Go with you?" I almost laughed out. "I have a wife and baby, remember?

"Sure," I continued seriously, "I feel deeply for the Russian Christians and I really admire the kids who are going. But I have a youth ministry waiting for me back in the States and I think that is where God wants me to be."

"I know," said Mac, "I realize it would be a crazy thing for you to do. But, somehow I just felt I should ask you."

He waved and headed down the courtyard. I stood there for a minute, the impact of the whole Moscow mission sinking into my muddled brain.

Really, I thought, they were crazy, just plain crazy!

"It is like the Children's Crusade!" I said to Rozanne later that evening in our tiny two-room apartment. She was ironing clothes on a board stretched between a chair and the bed. Anita was asleep in her crib. Rozanne's blond curls hung over her forehead, swinging back and forth as she vigorously pushed the iron.

"You remember the Children's Crusade," I said, trying to break her silence, "how all of those European children in the Middle Ages went to the Holy Land to free it from the infidels and were never heard from again?"

Rozanne's iron stopped suddenly, and she looked up at me asking, "Are you thinking of going with them, Nick?"

"Of course not," I stated emphatically, walking over to her and kissing her on the back of her neck, moist from the exertion of ironing. Rozanne was the practical one in the family. I was the dreamer. And after four years of marriage she knew me pretty well. But this was one time I was sure that her suspicions were wrong.

Little Anita was stirring in her crib and I walked over to the hot plate to heat her food. I looked back at Rozanne and again I thanked God for bringing us together. That was four years ago when I was an awkward young pastor in my first charge, a small Assembly of God church in West Long Branch, New Jersey. Fresh out of seminary, with nothing to my name except a few worn suits, I was certainly no prize. But we both loved the Lord, and this, we found, made up for everything else. Together, we sought His guidance and so far, He had not failed us. And His ways were good.

From the church, He led us into the Teen Challenge ministry in New Jersey where I had become director. Here again, I learned that every move God makes for us is a part of His educational process.

I had come from a conservative middle-class Italian background. I had disapproved of hippies, long hair on men, and people of low standards. But God had turned me inside out in Teen Challenge, teaching me new depths of compassion to where I realized that He loves each one of us. This included the drug addict nodding in the gutter who in turn is to be loved and helped by us.

After three years in Teen Challenge, I began to feel the Lord stirring me again. I sensed that He had something new for us on the horizon. What it was I didn't know, but I felt the strong guidance that we should prepare to leave. But it didn't seem logical.

"Wouldn't He first show us where to go?" I asked Rozanne.

"Maybe He wants you to be able to make the move as soon as it's time," she said with her usual matter-of-factness.

As I continued to pray that His will be revealed to me, I felt that He was asking us to make a proclamation of faith to show our trust in Him.

I took my first step in that direction by deciding to hand in my resignation at the next board meeting of Teen Challenge.

Now Rozanne and I began to get nervous. Stepping out in faith is one thing. The waiting is another. But we didn't have long to wait.

First came a phone call from my boyhood pastor who had introduced me to the living Christ as a real Person in my life when I was only twelve years old. It was in a small Pentecostal church in North Great River, Long Island. She was still pastor of that church

and called to ask if I could participate in a special service they were having there. Of course we agreed to go and, after the service, I mentioned my decision to leave Teen Challenge.

Pastor Virginia's eyes lighted. "Nick," she said, "there's a great revival going on here among young people and many are being saved. But there is a lack of Christian teaching in depth. Would you pray about coming out here to help us?"

I had a strong feeling during those following days that my next step on the Lord's pathway was being shown to me.

As Pastor Virginia suggested, I prayed about it. But a strange thing happened one morning as I prayed. The name of an evangelism school in Europe popped into my mind. Try as I might, I couldn't forget it.

I mentioned it to Rozanne for it was her brother, David, also a youth minister, who had told me about it. David leads an evangelical mission in Scotland which is headquartered in an ancient castle near Glasgow.

David Brett had attended this school of evangelism in Europe and was quite impressed with it. He had recently written us a glowing letter about his experiences there.

Now I was getting a strong, inner urging to attend it. When I told Rozanne, she was not exactly thrilled at the thought of it. Little Anita was only six months old and, furthermore, where would we get the money for the airfare? She did, however, agree to pray about it.

The feeling persisted—with me, not Rozanne. She said, of course, I should go if I felt it was the Lord's will. And we both were certain in that event that He would make it possible for me to go.

I began making the arrangements, half of me telling the other half that I was out of my mind. "You've finished Bible college," the first half argued. "This school in Europe doesn't even give credits. You will probably sit in a classroom with a lot of Jesus kids who have never had any formal Christian training!"

Despite all this and the fact that the next three-month session of the school was beginning in a few weeks, which usually meant it would be filled, I sent in my application.

God can work very fast. Back came my letter of acceptance

plus assurance that they would also have living quarters for my
family. But what about finances? Even though we had sold our car
and practically all of our belongings, we still had far from enough.
And then, mysteriously, practically without my asking, gifts of
money began to come to us from various members of our families,
friends, and even strangers. The strangest thing about it was that
we had told very few people of our need. Yet, all said that they had
an "inner urging" to help us.

Our plane was due to leave Kennedy Airport on January 2nd.
We stayed at my family's home in Islip, Long Island, for a few days
before leaving. These were highly emotional days. Even though my
dad and mother had emigrated from Italy and Dad had traveled
the world as a young seaman, the thought of their son, daughter-in-
law, and *piccolo bambino* going across the ocean was almost more
than they could bear. Yet, when they were assured that it was
God's leading, they understood.

As Rozanne, Anita, and I headed toward our departing plane
at Kennedy Airport, Mom and Dad were crying and my two
brothers stood silently at their side, holding back tears.

As our plane roared up into the night, I looked down at the
ribbons of light on the expressways surrounding the airport and
wondered which tiny pair of headlights would be their car, and
again I prayed for my family.

Now in Germany as I sat on the bed in our little room watching Rozanne fold the clothes she had ironed, I said to myself, "No,
this trip to Russia was not for me. I have too many responsibilities
—the work for which I was called in New York, my wife, and my
child."

Days melded into weeks at the school of evangelism. There
were four hours of lectures followed by two hours of work in the
afternoon. I washed dishes in the cafeteria and Rozanne helped to
clean. And more and more I heard the words "May Day Outreach." Each time, a surge of something I could not define arose
within me. And just as quickly, I would turn it off, much as one
would flick a switch to turn off the lights in a room.

But there came a time when that light switch wouldn't work
anymore.

They Must Be Crazy!

It was a bright moonlit night and I lay awake in bed letting my thoughts wander among the shadow patterns on the ceiling. I had been finding it difficult to sleep these last few weeks. There was so much to think about—going home, getting situated in my new ministry. Rozanne and the baby slept, their gentle sighing making a symphony of what I held so dear.

Where was the peace I had felt when I first dedicated myself to the Lord? Suddenly the truth began to flood through me and I shuddered at the realization. I had been putting God in a box. I wasn't allowing the Holy Spirit to have His way with me. I was telling Him He couldn't send me anywhere except back home close to my parents and brothers.

I realized that I must again totally relinquish myself to Him, to be willing to go wherever He sends me, even if it meant never going back to the United States—even if it meant going to Russia.

That night I slept deeply in the peace that only He can give, and I told Rozanne the next morning, "He wants me to go, Honey."

She was changing Anita. When the realization of what I had said came to her she stopped for a moment, safety pin poised in midair. Then she straightened and turned to me, her green eyes moist.

"Just make certain that it is God, Nick," she said, trying to smile.

That's all I needed. I sent in my application to the May Day

Outreach headquarters with the sixty-five-dollar fee. I also wrote Rozanne's father, Alan Brett, about it, but I could not tell my parents as they would worry so. Instead, I wrote them that I was taking a seventeen-day tour of Eastern Europe.

Rozanne's father is pastor of the Christian Center, a charismatic church in Morristown, New Jersey. Wisely, he did not try to influence me either way. He just wanted me to make sure I had considered all options and "above all," that I would "continue to pray for guidance." In the meantime, he, Mother Brett, and their little congregation in Morristown would be praying for us.

Rozanne and I needed those prayers the day my acceptance letter came from May Day Outreach. She interrupted her housecleaning to sit next to me on the bed and read the letter with me. It explained details and then ended with the impact of a live grenade being thrown into my lap. "We do not want you on this trip," it said in large type, "unless you are expecting to be arrested, mistreated by the officials, and have your property confiscated. . . ."

Rozanne gave a little cry. I jumped up, threw the letter on the bed. "Oh no," I said, "suddenly I have the feeling this whole thing is wrong."

One night after supper I was wandering the halls worrying over my predicament, when I saw one of our staff working at a typewriter.

"Doug," I said, sitting down at his desk, "I need help." He was the kind of friendly, down-to-earth kind of guy with whom one could talk frankly. "I'm not sure about taking that trip—sure that it is right for me."

He looked at me, his glasses reflecting the light of the bulb above him. "Have you prayed and felt the Lord's guidance to do it?" he asked.

"Yes."

"Well," he answered gently, his eyes looking at me steadily, "do you think the Lord has changed His mind?"

I didn't question my guidance again from that moment on.

Soon after that, the man who started it all came to our school. As Ted stood before us in the classroom, one could see nothing unusual about this slightly built, soft-spoken youth with his dark hair, brown eyes, and boyish face. He looked to be not more than twenty-five. Then he started to speak, and as he talked it became evident that Someone else was with him. There was a deep sense of the Holy Spirit in that room.

Ted explained that one day about a year ago he was in a study group similar to ours, praying for the Soviet Union. As he prayed he was given a vision. In it he saw a group of minivans filled with Christian kids crossing the Russian border. As he continued in prayer, he was shown that their witness was to be on May Day in Moscow's Red Square. There would be three purposes of the trip —One, to show the world through Soviet police reaction that there is no real religious freedom in Russia, the other to let Russian believers know that brother and sister Christians from the outside cared for them enough to risk imprisonment on their behalf. The third purpose was to witness to Jesus' love for all the Russian people.

The room was quiet as Ted continued. He pointed out that he felt that he had to check out his vision with Brother Andrew, "God's Smuggler," who had tremendous experience in bringing Christ's message to Iron Curtain countries. Ted had not met the

famous Bible smuggler and it was with trepidation that he went to Holland to see him.

He had heard of Brother Andrew's discerning eye. So many people on fire with emotionalism and cloak-and-dagger romanticism would tell Brother Andrew how much they would like to participate in his work. Brother Andrew has one test for would-be missionaries: He says to them, "Fine, I'll meet you behind the Iron Curtain in Poland . . . or Russia . . . and we can start from there." This seems to separate the men from the boys.

However, as Ted and Brother Andrew talked, they shared a closeness in the Spirit. And then the Dutch adventurer disclosed that he had shared a vision very similar to Ted's. Brother Andrew felt that the outreach should be May Day of 1973.

May 1, 1973—as I sat listening to Ted, I realized that date was only four weeks away.

As Ted continued talking in his low, earnest manner, I also knew that he was the kind of guy I'd follow anywhere.

He went on to say that one group of kids would fly into Moscow from East Berlin, another group would leave London in minivans, cross the English Channel, and travel up through Europe to Sweden, crossing into Russia at the Finnish border.

Ten of us were going from the school, but only two of us would be going with the London group. I would be one of those two.

Ted cautioned us to maintain secrecy. It would be difficult, he granted, with so many kids involved. But he felt that our keeping as quiet as possible about our plans would help to eliminate a "welcoming committee" at the Russian border.

One thing for certain, he emphasized—no Bibles, no tracts, nothing that would identify us as Christian evangelists could be taken across the border with us.

"But how will we witness?" was the question.

"We'll pray about that," was Ted's answer. An answer, we found, that we would hear again and again in later weeks.

We did pray, and insight came. Kids would be impressed with Scripture as they prayed. For example, one girl, while reading in the Bible, was particularly impressed with the phrase "raising banners to the Lord." Thus we knew that once we were in Russia we would make banners praising the Lord.

Another Scripture reference referred to "singing to the Lord" and we knew the Lord wanted us to sing His praises there.

We learned that my London group would rendezvous on April 19th to prepare for the minivan trek. Since school was over March 31st, that would give Rozanne, Anita, and me two weeks to spend with Rozanne's brother, David, in Scotland.

On Saturday, the 31st, after frenzied packing, we said good-bye to our friends at the school and the three of us flew to Scotland.

David, bright and merry-eyed David, met us at the airport in Edinburgh. It was so good to see him again. I owed him so much, for it was David who brought Rozanne and me together four years ago when I was that awkward, young pastor in New Jersey. It was David who married us on January 25, 1969. It was his first wedding.

Our remaining days together went by too quickly, and it was great listening to David's plans for his ministry in Scotland.

The day that Rozanne and Anita were to leave dawned cold and misty. We drove to the Glasgow airport in near silence. The moss green mountains and silver lakes of Scotland that passed my window would have been beautiful at any other time. I held Anita and couldn't resist burying my head in her golden hair as she cooed and laughed.

In the bustle of the airport, a little cloud of silence seemed to envelop Rozanne and me. We stood at the passenger line looking at each other without saying anything. I fought back the tears as I held Anita. The loudspeaker announced boarding time.

We embraced, Rozanne stepped back, looking at me with moist eyes. "Have a good time in Moscow," she said, her voice catching, then quickly took Anita from me and walked up the boarding ramp.

David and I rushed up to the observation deck. We could see Rozanne's plane loading. There she came with the baby and a stewardess helping her. I waved madly. She didn't see us and walked into the plane.

I felt empty inside. Until now my little family and I had never been separated. I was having just a small taste of what countless men and women have gone through since those days when the first apostles left home and family to witness for Christ. Today, I knew I would have made a poor apostle.

That night I sat down at David's kitchen table and started writing a letter to Rozanne. "Hey, mate," David laughed, "you're writing and she isn't even home yet!" I almost bawled.

Monday, David brought me to the airport. Another difficult good-bye. "God be with you," he said as we embraced.

The British Caledonia plane took me to London. There I caught the underground and headed for the address where Ted and the others in the May Day Outreach group would be head-quartered.

Finally, after much walking down misty streets, I found the number. It was the old vicarage which now loomed before me.

3

We Are One in the Spirit

I pressed the bell button at the side of the oaken door. The door creaked open, exposing a cheerfully lit hall and the brightly attractive face of a girl about twenty-one years old.

I introduced myself.

"Hi, Nick," she said with a smile, "we've been expecting you. I'm Jill. C'mon in and join the party!"

Inside the atmosphere was in complete contrast to the gloomy exterior. It was warm and buzzed with a happy expectancy. Some kids in jeans were lounging in the large drawing room reading, others talked in small groups or listened to tapes. Jill said she arrived from California a week ago.

"About thirty kids are here already," she said. "We're expecting the other twenty today.

"I'll take that back," she laughed. "Nineteen, now that you're here."

Ted came up and shook hands. "Nick, I'm going to have to leave shortly. Jill will show you around the house. Then I want you to place the people as they come. You know, set them up in rooms and stuff."

I gulped at this sudden responsibility, "Okay."

Right after Ted left, the doorbell started ringing every few minutes. Now *I* was the greeter. One after another they came, loaded down with backpacks, carrying bedrolls, and always a

Bible. Somewhere poking out between a bedroll or peeping out of a denim pocket would be a Bible.

Some were like twenty-one-year-old Jeff who hailed from Alabama. A tall, likable guy, he'd finished three years of Bible college, had been active at the 1972 Munich Olympics' Outreach to Youth, and now wanted to be where the action was. "Ah'm gung-ho for Jesus," he said.

There was even someone I had met before: Alice from California. A tall girl who still managed to look beautiful despite her preference for dungarees, Alice had long been active in Christian youth work.

And then there was Tony. In his forties, he was the "old man" of the group. His wife and daughters all were in some kind of missionary work. "My family is sold out to Jesus," he laughed. Tony used to be a barber in Lincoln, Nebraska. After he gave his heart to the Lord, he sold his business and his family has been living on faith. And, as he believed would happen, God continued to provide.

By suppertime most of the kids had arrived. We appointed some of them cooks and servers, others served on the clean-up crew. The chow line extended all around the house. Everyone had their own dish, cup, and other utensils. After supper, each washed his own dishes.

By this time, everyone had been settled somewhere. Sleeping bags were ready to be laid out in bedrooms, the drawing room, and library. And even though it was early, I was fatigued and looked forward to settling down in my own space for some much-needed rest.

I was laying on my bed listening to the singing drifting up from downstairs: "We are one in the Spirit . . . we are one in the Lord." Chris, a happy-go-lucky boy with bushy long hair, was playing the piano. Other fellows in my room were unpacking their gear.

There was a knock on the door. It was Sheri, Ted's wife. A sweet, attractive brunette with the same humble way of her husband, one couldn't help liking her immediately. She wasn't making

the trip with us, for Ted and Sheri were expecting their first child in August. Now, instead of her usual smile, Sheri looked concerned.

"What's wrong, Sheri?" I jumped to my feet.

"Trouble," she said, slumping down in a chair. "Ted just called; we can't get the minibuses for the trip." She explained that the man from whom we were renting them just learned that the vehicles could not be insured if they were going to Russia. He had previously rented minibuses to Russian-bound Bible smugglers and some vans had never come back. It was easy to imagine what had happened to them.

"Would you come downstairs and join us in prayer for this?" asked Sheri.

Some fifty of us gathered in the large living room, representing practically every Protestant denomination and Roman Catholic. As we sat together in prayer, a mystical warmth flooded the room, a glow, which I believe, was the Holy Spirit. From prayers for the insurance, our concern expanded—we prayed for each other, for our families, for the people of Russia.

A bond of love brought us together in one spirit. And, as we communed, time was forgotten, our separateness was forgotten.

When finally we ended our prayers by singing, "We are one in the Spirit, we are one in the Lord," two hours had passed.

That prayer brought us all together. Before we were a mixed group of some fifty kids from seven different countries—New Zealand, Ireland, Finland, Great Britain, United States, South Africa, and Australia. And, as with all new people getting together, there was a bit of a strain in conversations, an overpoliteness. After our prayer, tensions lifted and a friendly camaraderie blossomed. Coming together in prayer had welded us into a family.

Somebody laughed and said, "Say, we're kind of like Gideon's army."

"Right," we agreed, thinking about that tiny Old Testament band that freed Israel from her Midianite oppressors. Would we do as well in calling attention to the oppressors of Russian Christians?

The chatter rose in the room, and then came a hush. I turned to see that Ted had come back. There were tired lines under his eyes. "No," he smiled wearily, "nothing has changed with the insurance. But we'll just claim that it will come through. In faith we'll *believe* it.

"Now I've got visas to hand out," he continued. He had obtained one for each of us from the Russian Embassy in London. As he began passing them around, his brow wrinkled.

Some of the visas were dated April 29th, others April 30th. This wouldn't do. For us to cross the border together, the visas would have to carry the same date. "Just problem number 101," said Ted, resignedly. "I'll take them back to the embassy for correction."

Then Ted asked me to join him in the next room. I got there to find four other guys: Jim, Chris, Tony, and Ralph.

"Brothers," said Ted as he leaned against the paneled wall, "I've been praying about who the leaders of this group will be. Since we'll have five minibuses, that means five groups, and each needs a leader."

He looked at us for a moment. "The Lord has impressed it upon me that you five men will be the leaders."

I swallowed. I had already known I'd be a driver, but a leader?

"Now that I've given you the good news," Ted continued, "here's the bad news.

"Since you're leaders, you'll be singled out for interrogation if we get into trouble. And I must warn you, the interrogation could well be by the KGB."

I thought about the Richard Wurmbrand book I'd just been reading, *Tortured for Christ*.

"So in all fairness," Ted added, "I must ask if you really want this responsibility." He looked at each of us, one by one. All of us nodded.

Together we set up the fifty people into five groups. We tried to mix nationalities so each group would have kids from different countries.

"Each group must have a chain of command," said Ted. "If the leader is taken out of the picture, there must be someone right beneath him to take over, and so on."

The next day we met with our groups. I'll always remember that morning. It was sunny, unusual for London this time of year. We met in one of the downstairs living rooms. A gas heater in the fireplace produced a welcome warmth and the sun coming through the windows brightened the floral-design wallpaper and sparkled off the porcelain ornaments on the mantle.

For a few moments we sat there, some on sofas, others on the floor. Everybody, I noticed, seemed to be in their early twenties. We opened with prayer that our group would be a complete body of Christ, a real unity in that if one of us was in need, whether it be for help or correction, that another would see it and aid his brother or sister. We all agreed that in loving each other in Christ, we should encourage and correct each other for those two words mean the same when done in His Spirit.

Then each of us shared something about ourselves. Craig sat on the floor, leaning against the sofa. "Oh, wow," he yawned, shaking his head, "I'm still living on Pacific Coast time and it must be about 2 A.M. back there." He pushed back his long blond hair and then talked. Craig had been through the drug scene, the

revolutionary movement, and once helped try to take over the campus at Berkeley, California.

"You know, I'd got to looking at life," he said. "What was the sense of getting an education, making money—for what?" He said he was ready to join the Communist Party in the United States when someone introduced him to Jesus. Where he had previously turned off society because of its selfishness and materialism, in Christ's light he had found the "giving life" for which his soul was searching.

Craig would be our second in command.

Next in command was Rudy. His Mexican descent expressed itself in his flashing dark eyes, curly black hair, and Pancho Villa mustache. His white teeth sparkled as he smiled. "I would have gone the same way you did, Craig," he said, "but someone got to me early, thank the Lord." Rudy had been attending a Bible school in the San Francisco area when he got the distinct impression that the Lord wanted him to make this trip. "I wrote the London May Day Outreach headquarters," he said, "and they answered that they were completely filled.

"Well, the Lord spoke," he laughed, "and so I came anyway. When I got to England I called the headquarters and, lo and behold, someone had backed out. So here I am." Despite Rudy's ancestry, he couldn't speak Spanish, but he was fairly proficient in Russian.

The room was quiet for a moment. And then a beautiful British-accented voice flowed through the room. It was Gwendolyn, an attractive blond, with green eyes and typical British strawberry-and-cream complexion. She, too, could speak some Russian. "I'm a physiotherapist and work in London with young people who are spastics or suffer coordination problems." Gwendolyn said she had also felt impressed that she make this mission and had taken vacation time from her job for it.

Next to Gwendolyn sat Sheena. Her voice was beautiful, too, like a brook running down a glen in her native Scotland. She had been working with a mission in London. Long brown wavy hair framed a kind and friendly face. Sheena was eating a bag of potato chips and passing them around. When the sack came back to her the chips were almost gone. "Oh, good," she laughed, "now I won't have to worry about my diet." Sheena's rippling laugh made everyone brighten.

Half buried in a big chair in the corner of the room was Greg. A quiet, introspective guy, he always wore a strange-looking little button-down cap and even right now he had it on. Greg said he had heard about the trip from a girl in his church back in Illinois who had worked for Brother Andrew. Greg was a shy person and spoke so softly it was difficult to hear him. He felt a special burden for the Russian Christians because he was part Russian in ancestry and could also speak the language.

When Alan, a tall blond youth, said he was Scottish, Sheena laughed, "Oh, no, you're not!"

Alan groaned, "That happens all the time. You see, I'm from a part of the country which the Scots consider England and the English insist is Scotland." Alan had just turned twenty and was still in school. He said his parents had misgivings about his making the trip but had finally given their approval. "I couldn't think of a better way to enjoy my Easter vacation," he laughed.

Reggie, another Britisher, cleared his throat, "That's all right, Alan, whether you're English or Scottish, we love you just the same." Reggie was another one from a mission in London. He had an engaging smile under a mustache so bushy that his chin would seem to disappear under it. Reggie talked low with a very heavy British accent.

Next to Reggie sat Jill, the girl who had welcomed me to the vicarage the other day. She came from Southern California and, like Rudy, also made her trip here on faith. She, too, was told that the Outreach was filled, but she came anyway "because I knew the Lord wanted me to." Jill had long brown hair and still wore braces on her teeth which, when she smiled, only seemed to add to the sparkle of her expression. Jill's constant companion was her guitar. Even now, as she talked, she'd pluck a chord now and then as if to accent a point she was making.

Completing our circle was Cecelia, a college student from Denver, Colorado. An attractive brunette in hip-hugger jeans, she had given her heart to the Lord just a year ago and was still walking about three feet off the ground. She carried her Bible constantly and I had seen her reading it even while standing in the chow line. Cecelia shared special concern for Russian Christians. "Before I first learned there were so many in Russia suffering for Christ," she said, "I thought everybody there was a Communist."

As Cecelia finished speaking, I couldn't help but feel that the Lord had a special reason for each of us being here.

If I thought things were going to drag while we waited to take off, I was wrong. Right after lunch, Ted called the leaders to an upstairs room. When I walked in, the other fellows had already gathered there. Sitting on a chair in the middle of the room was a girl I had never seen before.

Ted turned: "Hi, late-comer, meet Pam."

I smiled and she nodded. Long, dark blond hair framed an angular face inset with piercing gray eyes. An air of mystery clung to her.

Ted explained that Pam worked with Brother Andrew's group and would explain how we'd pick up the Christian literature in Moscow, the material we were to distribute to the Russians on May Day. Pam shook her hair from her eyes and proceeded to talk with an air of crisp authority. "The literature—the Gospel of John—will have been smuggled in by the time you've arrived," she said, "and this is how you will pick it up."

She spread out a large map of Moscow on the bed and we all crowded around. The literature, she explained, would be stored by Russian Christians who would see that it got to Red Square on May Day. Some of us would be designated to make the pickups. Our people would wait on preselected corners and carry specially marked shopping bags which the supply agent would recognize.

Then Pam showed us how to make our own witnessing material. "It will be especially valuable," she said, "in case our people don't get through with the printed material." She held up two white paper crosses, each about eighteen inches high. On one was written the Russian figures for "Christ is risen!"; on the other were the letters which meant "Jesus loves you."

"Both are popular greetings among Russian Christians," she said. "These you can make in your rooms the night before May Day," she added. "Just be sure to bring enough paper and felt-tipped pens."

She tied a string to a cross and hung it around her neck. "And this is how you can show them on May Day," she explained.

Pam looked at her watch. "I have to leave now." She shook hands with each of us, saying "God be with you," slipped on her coat, and was gone.

Later I wrote Rozanne that I felt as if we had just participated in one of those dramatic briefing sessions on the "Mission Impossible" TV espionage show.

That evening all of us were enjoying "quiet time" downstairs. It was a typical scene these days in the old vicarage. One boy was

sitting on the floor sewing a button on his pea jacket, a girl was writing a letter, and, as usual, Jill was softly playing her guitar.

The doorbell rang, Jill ran to answer it, and in walked one of the most interesting people to join the trip. James was a former Trappist monk from Colorado who had heard about the Outreach, prayed about it, and felt led by the Lord to come. In his early thirties, he was a small-statured man who walked with a limp due to an early childhood illness. Despite his handicap, he was buoyant in spirits. One of the most unselfish men I have ever met, he was always looking for ways to help others. I never heard James criticize anything or anybody. I suppose you could say he was completely victorious in Christ.

That night he carefully unwrapped two art prints and showed them to us. "For some reason," he said, "I felt that there would be a use for these on the trip. Why, I don't know."

They were beautiful prints; one was an Indian brave on a pony, the other was a beautiful Indian girl. Both were done in the vibrant colors of America's Southwest.

Later, we were to learn how appropriate these prints would become.

By now everyone in the entire group of over fifty people related easily with each other in a casual camaraderie. No matter who one sat next to, a conversation flowed easily. Ted had come back from one of his many errands and we drifted into an informal worship session.

One by one kids would stand and pray, some of them sharing specific needs. At this, others near the one seeking help would gather around him in support. Particularly illuminating were the Scripture verses God had given many members of the group, verses that became promises in direct reference to our trip. If ever I felt we were doing something that was God's will, it was now.

And then a girl stood up. I remembered her arriving just a day before, asking to join us. She had a strange look about her as she stood in the middle of the room. Even in the lamplight, dark circles showed under her eyes.

"I have a prophecy that has been given to me," she announced. The room hushed as the other kids leaned forward expectantly.

"Someone," she said, looking around the room, "will die on this trip."

The girl's ominous words settled on us like a black cloud. The soft chords from Jill's guitar trailed off. The room became still. I could hear Ted, who was sitting near me, clear his throat. He climbed to his feet.

"I'm sorry," he said, speaking low, yet with emphasis, "but we can't believe that. We have prayed much about this trip and the Lord has never given me, or anyone else I know, that feeling."

He looked around at us. "But the Lord *has* shown that we *will* have a victory and that He *will* bring us back!"

Enthusiastic "Amen's" and "Praise the Lord's" resounded through the room. Then everyone broke into a chorus of: "All over the world, the spirit is moving . . . ."

Later, Ted counseled with the girl for some time. She agreed that since she didn't feel right about the trip, it would be wrong for her to continue with us. In what appeared to be happy relief, she left the next day bidding everyone well.

As Ted said afterwards, sometimes a prophecy or prediction is given to us that isn't from the Lord. That's why it's so important that we check these things out with Scripture and with other Christians to be sure in our hearts that something is really of Him before announcing it.

4

Race to Ramsgate

Easter Sunday, we all assembled in the drawing room for our morning service and communion. As we prayed just preceding communion, the Holy Spirit settled over that room. I began to feel sorry about the jokes I had made about the British way of life. For some time, in fact, I'd been critical of the English life-style. I knew that before I could come to Jesus in communion, I would have to ask all the British people in the room for their forgiveness. I stood and in a shaky voice announced this. A wave of love and emotion swept over the group. One after another, Britishers stood and also asked forgiveness for criticizing "you Yanks" and for "thinking our culture was so superior." An ocean of love and understanding flowed among us.

Then, apple juice and buns were brought out. We broke bread, giving it to one another, and drank His blood with the apple juice. I'll always remember this as one of the most beautiful and meaningful communion services in which I've ever taken part.

Whether it was the effects of our "confessional" or not, we'll never know, but that afternoon a most beautiful Easter present was delivered to us. It came in the form of word that the van owner had found another insurance company that would cover his vehicles. Hallelujah!

Tomorrow morning, Monday, April 23rd—M-Day minus 8—we would be on our way to Moscow.

Ted again went over our itinerary with us. Tomorrow, Monday night, we'd camp at the seaside resort of Brighton, then on Tuesday go to Ramsgate where a hovercraft would take us across the channel to Calais, France. We'd camp in Bruges, Belgium, on April 24th, Soltau, Germany, on April 25th, Copenhagen on April 26th, and sleep aboard a Finland-bound night ferry on April 27th. Then, on April 29th, we'd be somewhere in Russia!

We'd camp through Europe, Ted said. But once we got in Russia, the official Soviet agency, Intourist, through which our tour was arranged, would place us in hotels. "But that doesn't include meals," he added.

There would be no allowance for lost time on this trip, Ted emphasized. Our schedule had to be followed to the letter if we were going to make our target date in Moscow. One day's delay could throw our plans awry. "And this could happen," he warned, "even by missing one of our important ferry connections.

"We won't have to drive fast," he added, "but we'll be driving late into the day to make our mileage."

"And, please remember," he said, looking around the room at each of us. "We've done all we could to keep the purpose of our trip quiet. Let's be careful how we talk to strangers. We don't know who could be listening. The Soviet intelligence has a network that covers the world."

Sunday evening we drivers went down to Brighton to pick up the minibuses at the rental agency. Mine was a Ford Transit that seated twelve. The only thing that bothered me was its steering wheel being on the right-hand side. Would I ever get used to driving it?

Ted climbed into the van with me as we prepared to leave. "Okay, Nick," he said, "let's show the owner how well we can handle these things. I think he's a little nervous seeing how young we all are."

"Don't worry," I said, starting the engine. Through the rearview mirror I could see the owner standing at his door. The engine was cold and we were parked on an incline. I released the emergency brake, pressed the gas pedal, lifted the clutch. "Rrrrr-r-r. Chuggety-chug . . . chug . . . poof."

I restarted the engine. The same thing happened. Now I got

nervous. I could hear Jeff in the van behind me impatiently gunning his engine. I started the engine. Again, I stalled. Sweat beaded my brow.

"C'mon, Nick, let's get out of here," said Ted. "Give it the gun."

I did. The rear tires screeched and we laid rubber as we catapulted off. I still remember the look on the owner's face as his image rapidly receded in the mirror.

We rolled on toward London. Ted, in what I took to be Christian thoughtfulness, never said a word about our Cape Kennedy takeoff.

Monday morning dawned leaden. If we adventurers were pagans of old and looked to the sky for omens, we would have called off our departure. But the rain that began to fall didn't dampen anyone's spirits as we set to work putting the vicarage back into better condition than we found it. Kids scrubbed floors, polished windows, and vacuumed rugs.

And now came the hour. All fifty-one of us stood in a circle holding hands, praying for His guidance and protection.

Sheena, one of my group, prayed especially fervently for protection from accidents—I wondered if she had heard about my driving exhibition yesterday.

Finally, the vans were loaded. Tent rolls, backpacks, and sleeping bags were lashed onto the roof racks. Packed into suitcases and boxes were big sheets of white paper, innocent-looking enough to cross the Russian border but soon to be turned into crosses and banners for Jesus.

We were ready to go. Jim's van was ahead of us. It shuddered and took off. Now it was our turn. I pressed the accelerator, let up the clutch, and we pulled away.

Just as I was about to congratulate myself Gwendolyn squealed. My left wheels were climbing the curb. "Oh, Lord," I prayed silently, "please help me get used to the strange way these English drive."

Our caravan rolled on through the countryside, beautiful despite the rain and mist. The emerald hills rolled on before us. Our van was quiet and comfortable as we headed to Brighton. Some kids read, others chatted, Sheena was eating.

We joked about our van, tried to give it a name. Since it was green the "Green Turtle" was about the best we could come up with. We did better with Ralph's red van. That became the "Red Square."

Leading our caravan was Ted driving the blue van. Then came Jim, myself, Chris, and Ralph brought up the rear.

Ralph was there for a reason. He didn't have a roof rack, and thus he could keep an eye on our racks in case anything came loose. In fact, a half hour out of London, Ralph signaled me to pull over. My tarp was flapping and had to be retied.

At Brighton we pulled into the campground. The owner directed us to a large level area surrounded by trees and bushes where other tents had been set up. Another area was for cabin trailers where, we learned, many Britishers come to spend their entire vacations.

By now it was early evening, and still raining. But everyone had his job to do. Those who had just learned they were "cooks" unloaded the propane stoves and cans of corn, rice, and meat. It was a rather dismal chow line as we waited to dip into what soon would become a combination of corn, rice, meat, and rain.

Afterwards it was one of those times—too early for bed and too cold to do anything else.

"I know," said Ted, "we need a meeting." Once again his innate leadership showed itself.

But where to meet? The campground owners had nothing available. Then I remembered a beautiful old English pub we'd passed before turning into the grounds. We hiked over to it. "Certainly," said the proprietor, "we'll be glad to accommodate you." He ushered us to a large oak-beamed room complete with logs crackling in a cheery fireplace. We had a wonderful meeting getting dry and warm.

Finally, we reluctantly headed back to our tents which huddled like a herd of dismal elephants in a jungle rain. But they were dry inside. The tents had two compartments, each sleeping three people.

I lay there, the rain drumming on the canvas above, and I could sense the dampness seeping into my sleeping bag. Suddenly I became very lonely for Rozanne and Anita.

"What am I doing out here, anyway?" I wondered, wishing I'd stayed with my family and gone home to New York where I belonged. I felt more and more sorry for myself. Then I heard Craig's breathing next to me, and thought how much trouble he went through to join this crusade. I thought of Tony who'd sold his barbershop in what many consider middle age to give full time to his Lord. What a wonderful group of people. Now I felt badly that Rozanne couldn't meet them all. I knew she'd love them as much as I did. I dropped off to sleep dreaming that I was taking my wife around, introducing her to each one of the group.

I must have reached the forty-fifth person when I awoke to see gray light filtering through the tent fabric. I looked at my watch —6 A.M. The rain was still pecking at the canvas. My head felt like it was full of wet cement.

Would every campground be like this? I crawled out onto the submerged grass. Several other shadowy figures materialized in the mist, stretching and yawning. One looked a little like Tony. He looked terrible. "What's the matter?" I asked.

He smiled wanly, shook his head, and croaked, "Got a liddle cold; I be aldright."

I don't believe fifty-one colds were ever concentrated into a smaller area of England. We floated through the gloom to the rest rooms, shivering and sneezing. No hot water. I'd forgotten my electric razor and borrowed one. It conked out halfway through my beard.

"Who wants to go to the beach?" I called out in wild desperation. None of us will ever forget Brighton.

Breakfast was a big plastic box of cornflakes into which we dipped our bowls. Shredded wheat and other cereals were also available. I was ravenous. "Feed a cold," someone said.

"Okay, cold." I filled my bowl with cornflakes, put oats on it, then shredded wheat topped with sliced peaches, and plenty of milk.

Gwendolyn looked down at it. "No wonder all you Yanks are overweight."

Thank you, Gwendolyn. That was the first time I smiled that morning.

Soon it was time to break camp. My crew and I stood puzzling at the giant green tent and wondering how to take it down. We pulled stakes, loosened ropes, and it slowly collapsed. Folding it was something else. We vigorously attacked it, ending up with a giant ball of wrinkled canvas. Around it stood we four men, the pride of Texas, England, California, and New York, helplessly regarding what looked like a deceased dinosaur.

"Okay, fellows, move 'er over." It was Sheena and Gwendolyn. We watched in awe as two slight feminine forms unrolled the mess, smoothed out the canvas, and quickly rolled it into a neat package.

"Did you fellows watch carefully?" they asked.

We couldn't say a word. Women's Lib had struck again.

The day became even more complicated. Three of the vans had to go on to Crawley, a small city north of us, to pick up more supplies. The rest of us would clear camp, meet them in Crawley, and the five vans would go on to Ramsgate together.

In the meantime, Ted had to take a train to London to get our misdated visas straightened out by the Russian Embassy.

"Remember," he said as he left, "we must be at that hovercraft port at 3:30 sharp this afternoon. We've got our reservations and the tickets are paid for. I'll meet you there."

Before scattering, we all stood together for morning devotions, praying for guidance—we would need it.

By the time we'd cleared camp, it was close to noon. We began getting anxious. However, as we buzzed along toward Crawley, the drizzle dwindled and the sun broke out which took some of the pressure off. In Crawley we rendezvoused with the others in a big shopping mall causing no small consternation among the traffic bobbies as our vans maneuvered about like covered wagons preparing for an Indian attack. We were only trying to get them in proper order.

On to Ramsgate. Ralph was leading the way in the Red

Square. I noticed my gas getting low and signaled to stop for a quick fill up. It took some painful wheel twisting to get our van alongside the pump, and then we waited . . . and waited. The owner was busy on the phone and his conversation seemed interminable. Finally, he ambled out.

By now it was nearly 1 P.M.

More complications. Two New Zealand girls in our group were following our caravan in a station wagon which they had to drop off in a small town on the way. Then, Ralph of the Red Square had to stop in a town off the highway to pick up his wife. He told us to go on.

Now, I would be leading the pack. When Ralph turned off the highway, Tony came into my van. We looked at our watches, then at each other. It was 2:45. Ramsgate in forty-five minutes! Impossible! According to the map it would take over an hour.

"Oh, no," came concentrated wails from our kids. Tony turned to us. "Now look. We can't get panicky. Let's just sit quietly here, pray that we'll make it, and leave it to the Lord. God bends time for those who obey Him, you know."

We prayed, vowing not to speed, to obey all traffic regulations. We knew that if we broke laws it would show we were not trusting in Him.

We rolled on, not saying much, though many were silently praying. I could also hear someone nervously munching on potato chips. Everytime I'd glance at my watch, I'd catch Tony grinning at me out of the corner of his eye.

"What's the matter," he'd laugh, "don't you trust Him?" We kept brisk pace, no Indy 500 spectaculars or tire-screeching turns, but just purred steadily on. I was grateful the Lord was with me, for I'm sure that if I were alone behind that wheel, I would have had that gas pedal to the floor. We say we trust God, but under strained conditions our actions often show how shallow our faith can be.

"Look," someone exclaimed, "there's Canterbury." In the distance we could see the afternoon sun glinting off the famous cathedral's tower. How I wished we had time to see this spiritual center of England. I thought of Saint Augustine coming here from

Rome some fourteen centuries ago "to bring Christ to the island peoples." And now we were headed for Ramsgate, the place where he first set foot in England. In our little way, I mused, we were retracing some of his steps in bringing our witness to another people in their barbed-wire encircled "island."

The beautiful countryside rolled on. Sheep grazed on mossy pastures and we passed a farmboy shooing a herd of cattle.

I looked at my wrist again: 3:20 P.M. At that instant Tony pointed to a sign: RAMSGATE. Hallelujah!

In five minutes we reached the brink of a hill and, suddenly, below us was the hovercraft port with the sparkling channel spreading beyond it into blue infinity. Even from where we were we could easily pick out the giant half-boat, half-plane ferries. Fanlike propellors inside their hulls lift them slightly off the ground and water, the supporting air pressure being retained by heavy rubber skirts encircling the craft. Powerful propellors on top of the hovercrafts push them at high speeds.

Already we could hear the roar as one of them lifted slightly and floated toward the water. We charged down to the terminal, dust billowing behind us, expecting Ted and Ralph to be anxiously waiting for us.

But there was no sign of either. And Ralph had the tickets.

Tony and I rushed into the ticket office and explained our plight to the lady. She was very kind. "We've been waiting for you," she smiled. She checked with the hovercraft, then came back to us, her face concerned. "I'm sorry," she said. "They can hold only until 3:45. If you're not ready to board then, they'll have to leave without you."

The hovercraft was now revving its engines. The roar was overpowering. Tony and I looked at each other.

We walked out and passed word to the anxious faces leaning out of the vans. There was no need to say what we had to do. Everyone's head bowed.

It was now 3:40 and still no sign of Ted or Ralph.

Had they been in an accident? Was our crusade to end here?

5

Ferry Tales

The roar of the hovercraft heightened as its crew made last-minute preparations for takeoff. I couldn't stand still anymore. I grabbed my camera and headed up the hill, calling over my shoulder, "At least I'll get a picture of it before it leaves."

I was focusing my camera when a horn jolted me out of the road. I turned to see the Red Square hurtle by in a cloud of dust. It skidded to a stop at the ticket office and Ralph jumped out waving the tickets.

As I stood there gaping, another horn sounded. I stepped back again as a taxi rocked past. It squealed to a halt behind Ralph's van and out leaped Ted.

Forty-nine cheering throats vied with the roar of the hovercraft. "Step fast, step fast," called the boarding crew as they urged our vans up the wide ramp. It was just 3:45.

We settled in aircraft-type seats in the passenger compartment that encircled the deep hold in which the vans and a multitude of other vehicles were stored. With a tremendous roar, our hovercraft lifted slightly, moved onto the channel, and we started speeding to Calais. I expected it to be a smooth ride but it soon became quite bumpy. Whenever our ship hit a wave it would seem to go right into it.

The hovercraft bumped another wave and someone yelled, "Hey, they'd better fix this road; it's full of potholes!" A few of the kids had reached for the little paper bags by now. Two others argued whether one could call it being airsick or seasick.

In an hour we were driving our vans down the ramp at Calais. France looked as I always pictured it in my mind—quaint houses, men wearing berets, and lots of people on bicycles and motor-cycles. I was happy to learn that everybody in Europe drove on the right side, especially so after Ted came by while we assembled our caravan. He looked down at my left sidewalls which were badly scuffed by now. "You know," he grinned, "in England the people can always tell an American driver just by looking at his sidewalls."

"Okay, okay," I muttered as I climbed into our van, "at least we're back where everyone's normal." We took right off since we'd camp tonight in Bruges, Belgium, which was one hundred miles away and it was already nearing six o'clock.

We pushed on and as we neared the Belgium border, the sky-line of Dunkirk came into view. What a picture that very name brought to mind. Except for Tony, none of us had been born at the time of the dramatic evacuation from Dunkirk in World War II when 300,000 Allied soldiers were miraculously saved, mostly by small boats that scurried over from England. However, all of us were fascinated by its history.

"I'd like to see a shell crater or something," said Craig, study-ing the landscape whizzing by. "There you go," said Gwendolyn, pointing to a deserted house with its roof gaping. "A direct hit."

But we couldn't even slow down to look at anything, not if we were going to make Bruges by tonight. We reached the Belgian border and passed right on through with only the barest of for-malities as we did in France.

Long after darkness settled, we swung onto a four-lane super-highway. "Where *is* that campground?" muttered Craig. "It's al-most nine o'clock." Soon our caravan turned off the highway. Were we there? No. Word came back from the lead van that we'd gotten off at the wrong exit. Back again to the highway. "Looks like one of those midnight adventures again," said Gwendolyn.

Not quite. It was ten o'clock when we finally trailed into the campground. We assembled the vans in a big circle around our area, and left the lights on so we could set up the tents.

My tent team did double duty. Besides lifting canvas, Jeff and

Bill lifted spirits for they turned out to be a natural comedy team. The act started when we kidded Jeff about not being married yet. Jeff, who was all of twenty-one, said: "I'm willing to wait for the girl that the Lord wants me to have."

"Yes," chimed in Bill, "I've learned to do that, too. One just doesn't go around looking and dating. I've waited a long, long time and I'll just keep on waiting."

"How old are you, Bill?" asked Jeff.

"Eighteen," said Bill innocently.

Bill also did impersonations: John Wayne, Jerry Lewis, Ed Sullivan.

My cold was worse and I hit the sack early. The last thing I heard before dropping off to sleep was, "And now, folks, here's our really big sheow."

There was still one necessity four of our group needed. And that was smallpox shots. Without them, they couldn't get past the Russian border. The next morning Ted took them into a nearby town to find a doctor who'd give them. Meanwhile, we rested and had a quiet time around the beautiful little pond in the campground. Ted came back about 10 A.M. No luck.

"Well," he said, "it shouldn't be too long a trip today."

"Sure, sure," said everyone, nodding their heads knowingly. Tonight we must make Soltau, Germany, many miles away.

Back on the road we all decided one thing was certain. Our vans' gas tanks were too small. We had to stop and refuel every two hours. It was a major operation. Because of our group accounting procedure, we needed to pay only one gas bill at the stations. Thus, all five vans had to be filled from the same pump in succession. The confused station owner would scratch his head when we'd insist on this. However, there was another good reason. It gave fifty-one kids ample time to use the rest rooms. And any irritation suffered by the station owner was more than offset by his pleasure at seeing his wife sell fifty-one hungry kids candy bars and other snacks.

By now we were getting used to life on the move. The vinyl seats of the van were fairly comfortable and one could even stretch out in the back seat. Early in the morning we'd have a quiet time for meditation or Bible study; later we'd have discussions or often we'd all listen to a cassette tape by Christian teachers such as Brother Andrew.

But most everything we did we'd try to do together. We were careful to not separate into cliques. The kind of human weakness expressed in cliques can destroy the family spirit of any group. To avoid this we'd all change seats two or three times a day and thus rotate our conversations.

There was one who, up until now, did not change seats. Greg from Illinois. Every time I'd look back, there he'd be, huddled in the corner of the van, his little cap set low and his nylon jacket ballooning about him. Like the rest of us he was suffering from a cold but we sensed his main barrier was a deep, intense shyness. As I drove I noted the others always making a point to talk to him and include him in their conversations. But he'd usually just nod and smile.

The family spirit extended to everything including keeping an

eye on our van's shadow which we could see at the side of the road. It usually outlined our roof rack.

"Hey, Nick, our tarp is waving at us again!" would be the signal to pull over and retie the ropes.

We pulled into our campsite in Soltau, Germany at 11 P.M. that night. Yes, Ted, it was a short day.

Thursday, April 26th, our target: Copenhagen. On the way we stopped in a little German town with a beautiful little square. Ted found a doctor who would give the four in our group their necessary shots. Meanwhile we had lunch: a piece of bread with cheese, some chutney, and Kool-Aid. The Kool-Aid was stored in a picnic jug labeled "Adam's Ale."

Soon we were at the ferry that would take us to Denmark. Our van without the roof rack was able to go on with the regular autos but the rest of us had to wait. Meanwhile the kids in the first van had climbed to the aft top deck of the ferry, caught our attention, and started doing jumping jacks. At least we had some entertainment while we waited.

The hour-long ferry crossing found all fifty-one of us congregated in the large passenger lounge. The attraction: a beautiful smorgasbord, lush with Swedish meatballs, roast beef, chops in gravies, and all kinds of salads. We all stood about it quietly.

"Ted, I don't see a cashier," said Ralph. "I'll bet that food is included in our ticket." Inspired by his words several kids started edging for the trays at the end of the table.

"No," said Ted, "it can't be. It just looks too good to have been included in our fare." Finally, we found out—one had to pay the waiters.

Well, there was always rye bread, cheese, chutney, and Adam's Ale.

The trip gave the leaders a chance to talk. Everything seemed to be going well except with the kids in the Red Square. "It makes so much noise," said Ralph, "that we can hardly hear each other talk." He said that everybody was getting lonely.

Until now the Red Square had been traveling at the end of the line. So we decided to put them up in the middle so they wouldn't feel so lonely. "This way," said Ralph, "we can look out the back and see some familiar faces."

We all drove off the ferry except two fellows who didn't hear the landing announcement. I think they were still looking at the food. We held the vans and I ran back a quarter-mile to the ship to find them walking off with the foot passengers.

It's true what they say about Copenhagen. We entered the city after dark and it was a fairyland of lights. The song "Wonderful, Wonderful Copenhagen . . ." was all we heard in the van for the next fifteen minutes.

We camped outside of Copenhagen and Friday morning, April 27th, dawned to chill vapors rising from the ground. We were getting closer to the Arctic Circle. After our devotions, Ted addressed us.

"Brothers and sisters," he said, "today is going to be a long day."

"Oh, oh," said Bill, "what can *this* mean?"

"We're going to cross the Baltic Sea tonight on a ferry which goes to Finland. It's a six-hour voyage. We catch the ferry at midnight, so we're going to have to do a lot of driving between now and then to make it.

"Because," he emphasized, "if we don't make this ferry it will

throw our schedule off so much that we won't be able to make Moscow on May Day."

We packed as fast as we could and took off with our quiet time in the van lasting much longer than usual. We were all praying for the same thing—to make that ferry on time.

By early afternoon we were in Sweden. The countryside was charming with lovely evergreen woods, sparkling blue lakes, and little villas that looked scrubbed and polished. We craned our necks to look to the top of a cliff on which huddled the ruins of an old castle. We rolled through Stockholm around 9 P.M. and about all we could tell of this beautiful city was that it was very modern. "Someday," I thought to myself, "Rozanne, Anita, and I will see these cities as they really are. We'll explore their streets and find out what the people are like."

But right now our mission was Russia.

It was nearing 11 P.M. and finally we saw roadside signs picturing a ferryboat with arrows. We were nearing our destination. Hallelujah! Soon we rumbled along cobblestoned dockside streets. "Straight ahead" announced the ferry signs.

We pulled up on the dock and a cry went up from all five vans.

The giant white ship, all portholes ablaze, was slowly gliding away from the dock. Our information was wrong; it obviously left at 11 P.M. instead of midnight.

"Perhaps it's just turning around," ventured Cecelia.

As if to definitely refute her statement, every light in the entire dock area went out. The message was clear: "Closed; come back tomorrow."

6

On the Threshold

For one long moment we all sat transfixed. Then the deep-throated bellow of the departing ship's whistle broke the spell. Ted leaped out of his van and raced down the dock to where a man on a motorcycle had just ridden up.

Many kids, thinking they'd have a few minutes, made a dash for the dock rest rooms where pale bulbs still burned above the doors. It had been a long time since we had an opportunity to stop.

But in less than a minute Ted was back shouting, "Let's go!"

"Wait! Wait!" we cried, as we ran to the little building and frantically beat on doors marked *Herrar* and *Damer*. It turned out that the motorcyclist had told Ted that if we followed him to the next town "twenty minutes away" we just might catch another ferry.

The motorcycle roared off spitting blue flame and we lurched after it, tires shrieking. Suddenly I felt like I was driving the Grand Prix. We followed a narrow curving coastline road. My heart clung to my tonsils as we screamed around hairpin turns. Farmhouses, pine trees, and an occasional shocked pedestrian flew past us in the night like speeding ghosts. No one in our van said a word. Everyone was too busy praying and trying to keep from being hurtled to the floor.

Again, He was looking after us, for the lights of another town came into view. Soon we were at the dock, our guide on the motorcycle waving triumphantly. There it was, a giant white steamship just like the other ferry. Only this one was still tied up, her super-

structure sparkling with lights, and her boarding door open. Into
her massive maw streamed a line of autos, transport trucks, even
railroad freight cars.

· Praise the Lord!

As we waited in line to board, Craig pointed to a large cargo
ship docked nearby. On its bow was emblazoned a large floodlit
hammer and sickle. We watched it in silence; each of us, I'm sure,
was thinking about where we'd be the day after tomorrow.

It was our turn to drive aboard. After getting the vans
secured, we all headed for the ferry's grand salon. Ted hoped that
we'd find benches, sofas, and other warm places on which to lay
out our sleeping bags. We all looked forward to a restful night's
sleep while the ferry made its six-hour voyage to Finland.

But when we got to the salon it was wall-to-wall people. Every
seat on the ship seemed to be taken.

It was now after midnight.

We stood there, sleeping bags at our feet, droopy-eyed and
ready to drop from the long day's drive.

The dull drumming of the ferry's engines started. The whistle
bellowed. And what turned out to be the biggest party on the
Baltic Sea began.

Evidently this was the traditional Friday night way to enjoy
the crossing. Champagne corks popped, the nightclub band struck
up, and the bar suddenly disappeared behind a crowd of thirsty
people.

Some passengers had obviously started to celebrate before
boarding ship. One florid-faced man weaved past our group and
gave Gwendolyn a big wink.

"I wish," announced Gwendolyn, "that we had missed this
ferry, too!"

"C'mon," said Ted, "let's get out on deck."

We all filed out, carrying our sleeping bags like children taking their teddy bears to bed. A brisk Baltic wind cut across the
empty decks. The glowing heat lamps in the overheads didn't help
much.

But there were empty benches. Gratefully, I pumped up my
air mattress, crawled into my sleeping bag, and, with my back

facing the arctic wind, tried to fall asleep. It would be a long day tomorrow.

At 6 A.M. the ferry docked and we drove off into Finland, which was a strange new land for most of us. It seemed gray and cold. Rocks and shrubs lined the road as we drove toward Helsinki, the capital of Finland. By noon we were driving through its streets past clean-lined modern buildings of granite and we could see why it's called "White City of the North." Myra, a Finnish girl, had distant relatives in Helsinki who offered us sleeping space. This is where we would spend the night. Myra was "sure" she knew just where it was. We had a complete tour of Helsinki while trying to find it, through alleys, up and down hills. Finally, our caravan pulled over to the curb so we could talk. And that's when we discovered we had parked right near the place.

After getting settled, we discovered we could get discount rates at a nearby sauna. A number of us fellows went over to try what we had never experienced before.

It was wonderful to get heated up and dive into the swimming pool. Then we went into the showers. What luxury. The hot water seemed endless. Somebody next to me let out a little yelp, I turned to look and almost fainted.

Here came a woman, old enough to be my mother, walking through the shower room. She was an attendant, which we later discovered is a common practice in Finland and no one thinks anything of it. But we were stunned. We dashed to the locker room to get dressed. But since we were still dripping, the attendant kept right after us, trying to mop up.

As we walked back to the coffeehouse, everyone said their colds were much better. We weren't sure whether it was the benefit of the sauna, or the shock of the shower room.

Back at the house we had a meeting. It was already about 8 P.M. and we wanted to make it short since we'd be up at 4 A.M. tomorrow as we planned to be at the Russian border early.

First, we dumped all of our belongings on the floor of the big room and carefully searched for anything that might identify us as Christians. Bibles, prayerbooks, song sheets, crosses, books, all of these things would have to stay here at the house until we got back. Myra's relatives provided us with lockers where we could also store extra clothes and valuables that we didn't want to risk getting confiscated in Russia.

I felt strange giving up my Bible. It gave me an inkling how the Russian Christians must feel when they have to hide while holding worship meetings. Now I would have to carry the Bible in my head. I wished I had memorized more of it.

A Finlander, who had done much work among Russian Christians, came in to speak to us. "Love and humility must be your guide," he emphasized, pointing out that if we were on this trip just so we could boast about "witnessing" in Russia, the Lord would see our motive and not honor our goals.

Now we were spurred to perfect our Russian salutations with which we'd greet Moscow people on Red Square in words and on our banners and crosses: CHRIST IS RISEN and JESUS LOVES YOU.

Our Russian linguists in the group huddled together and came

up with the words. " 'Christ Is Risen' would be pronounced: *'Christos voskresen,'* " said Rudy.

"Christos voskresen," we all echoed.

"And now, 'Jesus loves you.' This one is a bit more difficult to pronounce," Rudy said, "but let's try it: *Eezoos lie-oo-bit vas."*

"Okay, can you say it?"

"Ee-zoos lie-oo-bit vas."

"Good! Let's say them again."

It was like the scene from "My Fair Lady" with Professor Higgins teaching Eliza Doolittle. Soon the phrases flowed off our tongues easily.

Suddenly, the chatter ceased. It was as if the very act of speaking these greetings brought home the seriousness of our mission.

"Let's pray for God's protection and guidance," said Ted. One by one, we stood and expressed what was in our hearts. Occasionally someone would give a message in tongues. Another would interpret. Usually these messages were confirmation that God was with us.

A warmth flowed through the group as we worshiped. People prayed for each other. I was surprised and touched when someone prayed for my family and that I wouldn't miss them to the point of discouragement. I realized then how much I had been talking about Rozanne and Anita.

Perhaps this worship was particularly meaningful to us in that we realized it would be the last time that we could pray openly together as a group. Ted cautioned us that even in our hotel rooms we were not to pray out loud.

"Remember," he emphasized, "when asked, just tell people that we are students touring Russia."

I thought to myself that in the official Soviet mind, this is all we would be anyway, since they do not recognize God.

"We'll be asked many questions," Ted continued. "And our answers must be led by the Lord. That's why it's so important that we keep in constant prayer, mindful of His guidance and wisdom. We must believe that when questioned, we will be given the right words to say at the right time."

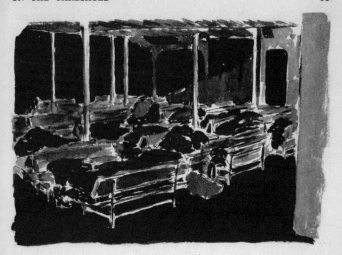

Our meeting lasted longer than we expected and it was after midnight when we finally dropped off to sleep. As I drifted off, I could dimly hear our comedy team: "Goodnight, Jeff. Goodnight, Jim. Goodnight, Bill."

Four o'clock came too quickly. No one talked much as we climbed into the vans. The five minibuses stood quietly on the dark Helsinki street for a few minutes as each group held its own devotions.

Then Ted beeped his horn, we started our engines, and headed for Russia.

We had traveled about ten miles when Ted pulled over, his hand waving out of the window for us to stop. He came back to tell us that one of the girls in his van had forgotten something at the house and they would go back while we waited. As we sat there, the sky began to lighten before us. On the far eastern borders of vast Russia it was already daylight.

I turned to the group. "Is everyone sure that we have nothing on us that would identify us as Jesus people?"

Everyone looked again, checking pockets, the floor of the

van, the glove compartment. "Oh," groaned Sheena, "I'd forgotten." She held up a ballpoint pen she found in the bottom of her purse. On it was inscribed: *For God so loved the world that He gave His only Son.*

"Maybe we can scrape off the words," said Craig. With a knife he began working on it. But it looked too obvious that a message had been removed.

Alan laid it on the ground in the field next to the road. "Maybe some nice farmer will find it," he said.

Were we becoming too careful? I wondered.

At that moment Ted came back. His face was serious as he walked up to us. "Back at the house they told us that as our vans pulled out this morning, someone was watching us from a nearby window with binoculars."

A chill came over us and it wasn't the brisk morning breeze.

We took off, stopping only at a gas station which we were lucky to find open this early. As we waited at the pump, I noticed Sheena moving next to Greg who still hadn't said much since we left London.

"Say Greg," she said, "now that we're this close to the border, how about teaching us a little Russian? Like 'Good morning,' for example?"

Greg's face brightened. "Oh," he said, "I don't know a lot, but I can help you with that. It's *dobroe utro.*"

"*Dobroe utro,*" repeated Sheena slowly.

It was good to see this little tableau. Sheena was wiser than I thought. In asking Greg for help, she knew that she'd be helping him emerge from his backwardness.

As we drove on, the farms became fewer and we knew we were nearing the border. Then Craig pointed. A guardhouse was ahead. Were we at the Russian line? We slowed, then saw the Finnish flag, with its blue cross against a white field, flying over it. One guard was manning the little house. He smiled, stepped over to the vans, checked us through, and waved us on. We all commented on how informal he seemed to be.

"Well," laughed Greg, "who worries about people escaping into Russia?"

We rolled on through rolling hills covered with evergreens. This evidently was a "no man's land" between Finland and Russia. The sun was up now and the pine-scented air seemed to sparkle. We were singing softly "Praise ye the Lord . . . ." when the words suddenly died in our throats.

Down the road, majestically waving above the trees, was a giant crimson banner bearing a gold hammer and sickle.

7

The Curtain Parts

"They look so young!" gasped Cecelia.

A long red-and-white-striped pike barred the road. Behind it stood three soldiers, one carrying a machine gun. They *were* boyish looking with their close-cropped hair. But everything else about them was coldly militaristic with their neat, tan uniforms over well-polished boots. Serious eyes studied us as we approached.

Van by van we were inspected. The procedure was always the same. Two soldiers would come up to the driver's window while the third man with the machine gun would stand in the rear as if he were covering the operation.

As they began to approach us, I could feel the tension mount in the van. I turned to Greg: "What Russian greeting should we give him?"

"How about 'Jesus loves you'?" someone said dryly.

"This is no time to be funny," I snapped. Immediately I was sorry. We were all nervous and the humorist was only trying to relieve the strain.

The soldier reached my window, saluted and asked: "Passports, *spasibo*." *Spasibo* was one word I knew; it means "thank you."

I handed him our bundle of passports with a hearty *"Spasibo."*

He opened them one by one. With each, he'd study the photo, ask where the person sat, look at them, then nod his head.

It was eerie, being studied like this.

Finally, he completed his inspection, bundled the passports together, and handed them back to me.

"Spasibo," I said.

He saluted and went on to the van behind us.

It took a half hour for them to check the caravan. Then, one walked into the guardhouse and picked up the phone, evidently alerting someone down the road.

As the others stood nearby, we'd try to catch their eye, but it was impossible. We wondered if we did, would they ever smile?

The other guard stepped out of the house and waved us on. As we drove off, no one said a word. It was as if we all were wound so tight we couldn't speak.

Then someone called out, "Look at that little tree!"

We turned to look in the forest. A small oddly twisted fir huddled under giant trees, spotlighted by a ray of sunlight which streamed down upon it. The little fir had grown into the shape of a cross.

It was as if the Lord were reassuring us: "Lo, I am with you always."

We drove on through dense forest, then broke out into an open area of completely raw earth. It looked so strange we hesitated for a moment. A swath of earth, fifty-feet wide, devoid of tree or blade of grass, extended on both sides of us as far as we could see. A tower loomed in the distance. Someone said this border strip was so heavily mined that a person walking across couldn't help but be blown up. Moreover, every square foot of the strip was under close observation by tower guards armed with heavy caliber machine guns.

For a moment, we were caught by the ominous presence of this "death strip," but soon it was behind us. Gwendolyn exhaled in relief and said, "Well, I'm glad *that's* over."

"What's over?" I asked.

"The border inspection," she said.

I pointed down the road ahead. A stone tower rose above the trees. Beneath it squatted a huge customs house.

"You mean we've got to go through this all over again?" she gasped.

"Like we've never been gone through before," said Reggie, who had heard about the process.

Men in blue coveralls met our caravan and waved it over to a building. Two heavyset grandmotherly type women came up smiling.

"Maybe they're our guides," ventured Sheena.

"I hope so," said Cecelia, "they look so nice."

But all they wanted to see was our health cards.

Later we learned they had given Ted quite a scare. As they approached his van, one said, "I suppose you know that we realize you people came from London?"

Ted said that he froze inside. "I expected them to tell me the address of the vicarage."

As it turned out, there had been a smallpox scare in London two weeks ago and all the woman meant was that they had to be particularly careful that everyone in our group had their innoculations.

If Ted hadn't made sure everyone had their shots, several would have had to leave us here.

Our minibuses were then ushered up to another large building. This is where they were given the third degree.

As we watched, each van was driven over a deep pit. A man below armed with a thin metal rod, carefully prodded into every section of the undercarriage like a dentist checking teeth for cavities.

Another man, with a periscopic device, investigated the interior of the gas tank. They removed the horn button and looked under it.

When two blue-overalled men began removing the door panels I chilled. What if the previous renter of this minibus had overlooked one of his Bibles?

Now they moved to the van's contents, food and luggage. As one peered inside a box of cornflakes, good old Gwendolyn came up with, "Does he think it's Cracker Jacks and he's looking for the toy?"

While all this was going on, I noticed an important-looking uniformed man come up and talk to the crew which was examining us. As they talked, he kept watching us, and of course, I couldn't understand a word.

I became frightened. I was sure that he was telling them that we had the Bibles somewhere. Of course, they recognized the vans!

"C'mon, Nick," I said to myself, "don't get paranoid."

I couldn't help but think of Brother Andrew and the others who actually smuggle Bibles through the Iron Curtain. How do *they* feel when undergoing this inspection? I turned to Ralph, "Only God could get a Bible through this."

"Well, I don't know how anyone could live under a system like this," said Ralph. "We've been in Russia only about an hour and already I feel like I've been through a century of the Inquisition."

Finally, we were cleared, and we took off. We'd gone only a little ways when we spotted a turn-off down the road and Ted motioned for us to stop there. "A good place for lunch," he called back.

Suddenly, a jeep with four soldiers pulled up. The two in back were women. They motioned we couldn't stop there. We pointed to our mouths. "Okay, okay," the driver said. As they pulled away, we noticed the two women craning toward us, studying us very carefully.

All the kids tumbled out. One got the soccer ball and we started playing soccer right on the road. Then we had our usual repast of bread, cheese, and chutney.

As we continued on through the Russian countryside, we could see people ahead and wondered if they, too, would be cold and stiff like the border guards.

What a difference! As our little caravan wound through the village, men, women, and children waved and smiled. Children ran toward us.

Most of the women wore kerchiefs around their heads babushka style and they all seemed to be very heavy. However, the young girls looked quite sharp and attractive and some of the fellows loudly commented on this.

"Disloyal!" snorted Gwendolyn.

A group of boys on bicycles started wheeling in and around our caravan. "Chewing gum! Chewing gum!" they pleaded. We had chewing gum in the luggage but, for some strange reason, did not feel led to give it out. Later we learned there was good reason for our not doing this.

Now we began to see large banners along the road, evidently in honor of May Day, just two days away. Greg translated the words on them: ALL GLORY TO LENIN. ALL GLORY TO THE U.S.S.R.

"And praise to the Lord!" shouted Sheena.

As we continued, the land changed in character as the Gulf of Finland began to cut in toward us. Now it was becoming an area of vast marshes.

"Oh, oh, what's this?" asked Alan. A soldier with a machine gun stood by the highway ahead of us. He motioned us to slow down.

It turned out to be one of the many checkpoints that guard the Russian highway system. These consist of a guard tower housing a small contingent of soldiers.

In this case, the tower had evidently been alerted by customs that we were on the way, as the soldier motioned for us to slowly continue. As we passed, a policeman counted every passenger in each minibus. We laughed about this later; what would have hap-

pened if one of us had been stretched out flat on the seat asleep?
Would they have sent out an alarm for the missing student?

Now we approached Vyborg, an ancient city along the Gulf
of Finland. As we rolled into its cobblestone streets, we passed
some of the sixteenth-century fortifications that are still standing.
Again, people on the streets smiled and waved, but they were not
as exuberant as in the small towns.

We had to find the Intourist office. Intourist is the official
Soviet tour bureau through which we arranged our tour in London.
Now we had to check into the local office for our tour vouchers
and to pick up our guides.

As we continued through town we were impressed by the fact
that there were no advertising signs. "Simple," said Reggie, "there's
no reason to advertise. No competition. For instance, there's one
soap available, and if you don't like it, tough."

Our caravan pulled up to a large building bearing giant
painted portraits of Lenin and Karl Marx. This was the railroad
station and also the location of the Intourist office.

We pulled the vans into the parking area. Ted and some of
the kids went into the Intourist office, others said they'd stay by
the vans, and the rest headed for the "bank" to change their money
into Russian currency. Sheena said she heard that Russian ice
cream was very good and went looking for a cone.

I went to the bank. Actually, it was a room in connection with a souvenir shop. When I gave them my three dollars, all the money I had, they gave me back two rubles and twenty kopecs.

Downstairs was a room full of free literature. Most kids picked up everything they saw. Soon we Christians were carrying more Communistic propaganda than *Pravda* could publish in a year.

I stepped into the train station and was trying to make out the hieroglyphics on the schedule when one of the girls, who had been with Ted in the Intourist office, ran up to me.

"We'd all better pray," she whispered, "because it doesn't look as if they want us to reach Moscow."

An uneasy feeling began to creep over me. I stepped outside and joined Jeff, Craig, and Ben who were standing on the building steps. I told them what I had just heard. We all started to shift nervously, especially since some people across the street seemed to be watching us.

And then it happened.

Two tough-looking teen-agers stepped across the street and walked over to us, snickering. One boy, heavily built with close-cropped hair, suddenly reached into his pocket and brought out an egg. He held it in his hand in front of him, gently bouncing it and laughing softly as if to say, "This egg is for *you*." All the while he kept saying something under his breath. We couldn't make it out. The other boy stood by smiling with a knowing look. Then we heard them spit out sardonically, "Christos voskresen . . . Christos voskresen!"

8

The Eyes of Russia
Are Upon Us

Finally, the twosome turned and sauntered away as we watched in shock.

"Wow!" Jeff exhaled. "What do you think *that* meant?"

We hurried back to the vans where, by now, the others had assembled. Soon Ted walked up with a strange young man.

"Meet Viktor," said Ted. "He will be one of the two guides that Intourist has assigned to us."

Maybe the encounter on the corner made me overly suspicious, or perhaps it was the cut of Viktor's black double-breasted suit, or the military look of his black turtleneck sweater. But as we shook hands, his intelligent-looking gray eyes boring into me, I wondered what rank Viktor held in the KGB, the Russian secret police.

Within a few minutes we met our other guide. Nadjina was an attractive brunette who would look at home on the streets of New York City. Smartly dressed in slacks, turtleneck, and a leather jacket, she swung a tooled leather handbag as she walked up to our group. Curly black hair framed a small face that would have been pretty except for a certain pinched sharpness. As Ted introduced us she acknowledged our hellos with a quick nod and faint smile.

"Okay," Ted called down the line with what sounded like forced cheerfulness, "let's get this show on the road." As we

73

boarded, Nadjina climbed into the front van and Viktor stationed himself in the rear vehicle.

Ted, who had remained outside, now hurried up the line of vans. As he came to us, he thrust his face into the window and hissed, "Pray like mad! It looks like they don't want us to reach Moscow!"

As we started rolling, the van was quiet for a moment. Then, as our spirits released, everyone started talking at once.

"Do you think they *know?*"

Soon Ted signaled for us to pull over. It was time to refuel. But what a gas station! We were to learn that it was typical of all the gas stations we'd see in Russia. As we drove under the large overhanging roof, it was like stepping back into 1925 in the United States. The small service building had been covered in tile, most of which had long fallen off. Inside sat a plump woman who controlled the pumps with a switch. We'd insert the hose into our tank, nod to the woman and when we felt that the tank was full, signal her to stop. As our caravan refueled in its usual one-by-one fashion, a taxicab pulled up to the other pump. The driver signaled the woman, then stood with his hands in his pockets as he studied our group in curiosity. Suddenly gas spurted out of his tank as it overfilled. We yelled to him and he stared at us uncomprehendingly. Finally, it dawned on him and he spun around, shouting to the woman to turn it off. He quickly paid his bill and, in obvious embarrassment, leaped into his cab and sped off.

This taxi was one of the few cars we saw on the highways of Russia, because, Tony told us, few Russians can afford cars. We did occasionally pass a passenger bus lumbering along the road. Old and decrepit and identified only by a number printed on its dusty, rusty side it would be packed with people. Suddenly, I became very homesick for a Fifth Avenue New York City bus emblazoned with its colorful advertising banners.

One of the Russian buses preceded us into a highway checkpoint and we watched a policeman board it. He made his way up the aisle, checking every passenger's papers. Another man, armed with a machine gun, walked past our caravan, asking each driver

how many people were in his vehicle. What would happen, we wondered, if somewhere along the line one of us accidentally gave him a wrong figure?

After the checkpoint, we started seeing more people walking beside the road. Some of them, particularly the young people, on seeing our foreign license plates, would smile and wave. We'd wave back. Somehow the cheerfulness of their greetings overcame the pall of the security-conscious atmosphere under which it seems all

Russians must travel. However, as the population seemed to thicken, we saw less and less smiling people. Now most of the people we saw wore dour expressions, as if the sun had stopped smiling for them. We began to pass factories, large dark masses on the horizon studded with smokestacks. It was evident that we were approaching a large city.

"Yes," said Craig, checking the map, "we should soon be in Leningrad."

Leningrad! Russia's second largest city, surpassed only by Moscow. I remembered from history how Peter the Great had in 1703 ordered this city built as a "window looking on Europe." Ten years later when it was completed, he moved his capital to here from Moscow. Then called Saint Petersburg, it became one of the world's most brilliant cultural centers. Famous Italian and French architects had planned Leningrad, and now as we rolled along its broad avenues we gasped at its spacious, classical beauty.

Graceful bridges carried us over rivers and canals and we were reminded that Leningrad is Russia's main seaport. Soviet naval ships were moored in the river, their decks lined with sailors in dark blue uniforms, and many sailors strolled the streets. We surmised they were in port for the upcoming May Day Parade.

We followed a wide boulevard called the Nevsky Prospekt to the center of the city. Our caravan pulled into an immense square where we all got out to see the Czar's Winter Palace, a magnificent collection of massive stone buildings.

Viktor told us that in the old days, a crowd of poor people walked to the Czar's gates to beg for bread. As they approached, Cossack troops rode into their midst and slaughtered them. Viktor spoke as if this incident alone could well merit the Revolution. But as he talked, I thought of all the bloodshed of that Revolution and the continuing suppression in its name. I couldn't help but think of Christ's words: "For all those who take up the sword shall perish by the sword." Today, millions of people continued to die, not as much in the physical but in the spirit as new generations of Russians suffer oppression under a different name.

The force with which the "new order" drives its traditions home was everywhere in the resplendent red banners. In fact, the

city seemed a mass of red, interrupted only by giant portraits of a sinister-looking Lenin. And the goal of our trip was again brought to mind as we passed a massive reviewing stand from which notables would soon be watching the May Day Parade.

"Only a day after tomorrow," I thought. "Will we be watching the parade in Moscow?"

Rudy had settled back and was enjoying the sights of Leningrad when suddenly he grabbed my arm. "Look," he cried, pointing to the top of a Romanesque building ahead.

On its roof stood two men. One was flashing a light semaphore message to our lead van. The other stood peering at the van through binoculars.

In seconds we had passed the building. Rudy turned to me, "Did you see what I saw?"

"Yes," I said quietly, "those two men."

Neither of us were able to say anything for the next several minutes. So much had already happened on our first day in Russia that talking seemed superfluous.

Gradually, the spires of Leningrad fell behind us as we drove into open country toward Novgorod where we would spend the night. Dusk was falling as we passed through villages. Many people were strolling along the road. Tony said this was a typical pastime here among families and was also a way young men and girls would spend their dates together. We all thought it was a rather nice custom.

But we also continued to see the poverty—in the small rude log houses, in women bent under yokes as they carried water. And we also saw hopelessness in many men who were obviously heavily intoxicated by, we assumed, too much vodka. Usually, these unfortunate souls would be supported by companions as they struggled along. I had read that the consumption of vodka is causing concern among Russian government leaders. Obviously, "the perfect social order" does not assure everyone peace of mind.

Even in these small villages, the civic building would be draped with red flags and the ever-present portrait of Lenin which led me to believe that he is being deified.

"Big Brother is watching you," laughed Gwendolyn. But I didn't laugh—the two men on the building roof were still too fresh in my mind.

Ted signaled for a "relief" stop, but I didn't get a chance to speak with anyone in the lead van about the signals we saw in Leningrad and made a note to check this out when we reached Novgorod.

As we approached this medium-sized city which dates back to the Middle Ages, its onion-domed cathedrals slowly rose above the horizon. By now it was late and we said little as we drove to our hotel. All of us were very tired. However, after we unloaded, I did get to Jim who was in the front van. I told him what we had seen in Leningrad.

"No, I didn't notice anything," he said, trying to recall the spot I described. Suddenly, his eyes widened: "Say!" he exclaimed. "I remember! It was right at that spot that Nadjina made a funny movement with her hands . . . as if," he continued, his voice far away, "as if she was signaling someone."

I wanted to also check this out with Ted, but he was tied up making room arrangements for us. Dinner was announced, and now we were given another surprise. Though our tour covered only bed and breakfast, Intourist now insisted that it included all our meals. The point was that we would take these at the time and place they specified.

It was a mixed blessing. On one hand, who could complain about free meals. On the other, why did they want to do this? To make it easier for them to keep us under surveillance?

As I trudged up the stairs carrying my duffel bag, all of the odd things that had happened to us on this first day in Russia suddenly seemed too much.

"Nick," I said to myself, "you're getting paranoid. There's a reasonable explanation for everything. You've been seeing a plot in every coincidence. You're tired and need your rest."

I leaned against the door to my room. It was stuck. Up hurried a beautiful little old woman who was in charge of this floor. She was a roly-poly grandmother type whose sincere warmth and wish to be of help made me feel very foolish about finding a spy under the rug.

She made me feel so much at home I was reminded again, with very few exceptions, how wonderfully friendly the Russian people were, with no apparent antagonism for the West. So often we think of Russians as all being hard-bitten Communists when actually, only a tiny percentage of the population belong to "the Party."

This smiling "babushka" reminded me that dinner was ready downstairs in the dining room. As I approached the table, it was quite a sight after the hard day's drive. Spread out before us was dark Russian bread, thin-sliced meats, a ground meat mixed with other ingredients, and on top of which was a fried egg, french-fried potatoes, and peas.

As we prepared to dive into the repast, I automatically looked to Ted for the blessing, then remembered—*not here*. And so, all of us silently gave thanks to Him in our hearts.

After dinner, Viktor announced that we would sightsee in Novgorod tomorrow. By this time it was nearly midnight and I was ready for bed despite the blandishments of the stand in the lobby where one could buy postcards, souvenir jewelry, plus, yes, portraits of Lenin.

In my room, I started a letter to Rozanne. I wrote her about the pressures we were beginning to face and finished by writing that we "were praying" that we would get to Moscow.

"Praying"? What if they censored our mail? I folded the letter and stuffed it in my suitcase. As I sat there, I longed for my Bible. Suddenly, I desperately needed it for solace and comfort. But it was far away in Helsinki. Now I began to understand how a Russian Christian felt. I turned to the Scripture I had memorized and contented myself with going over it again and again.

The Embalmed Religion

"Be careful what you say—that man has been watching us."

It was Sheena who had slipped up to me as I stood in the hotel lobby. It was early Monday morning, April 30th. I had been standing there, waiting for the others of my van's group to gather for our morning tour of Novgorod. But my mind was far from the impending tour. Instead I was thinking that tomorrow was May Day. By this time tomorrow we should be well on our way toward Red Square.

I looked up to where Sheena had pointed. I had seen the man before. A heavy-set Russian in a tan trench coat, his eyes almost hidden under a bright green felt hat.

And now I almost laughed. If anyone acted out a caricature of a Russian spy, it was this individual. As he held up a newspaper and pretended to read it, I watched him edge over to one of our groups obviously trying to overhear the conversation.

"Well," I laughed, "in that green hat nobody could call him a plainclothesman."

By this time our group had assembled and we stepped outside and gathered on the hotel lawn. A small group of policemen who had been standing across the street now started toward us.

"Maybe we should get off the grass," said Rudy.

We quickly moved and the police walked on past us. At the same time, three uniformed women slowly walked past from the other direction, then stopped fifty feet up the street and stood watching us.

Sheena gave a nervous little laugh. "Maybe they've decided to search our luggage."

"Yeah," Rudy laughed nervously: "I hope no one took any hotel towels with them."

Just then Ted came up. "Say, Nick," he said, studying a list in his hand, "you folks didn't have a guide yesterday."

"No," I answered, starting to say that we'd be very happy to keep it that way, when he added, "Fine, then you'll have Nadjina today."

"Thanks, Ted," I answered wryly, "I don't know what we've done to deserve it."

"A little rain must come into everyone's life," he laughed. Instead of rain, it was a little black cloud that came with Nadjina when she climbed into our van.

We began our tour of Novgorod feeling as if a policewoman was taking us to jail. Her manner continued to be crisp and sharp. Moreover, she rarely volunteered anything about the sights. Our questions met clipped retorts, or worse. When one of the girls asked a simple question about the Russian government, Nadjina snapped, "*Why* do you want to know *that?*"

By prying and pulling, we did learn that Novgorod is one of Russia's oldest cities and was a major commercial and cultural center of medieval Europe. Because of its beautiful architectural monuments, it was called the "museum city" until World War II when it suffered great damage. However, from what we could see, it had been rebuilt extensively with little trace of its former devastation.

Our caravan wound through the streets and then pulled up to a massive walled fortress. And then Nadjina said what many in our group later claimed was her nicest statement of the day.

"I will leave you now and a local guide will take over."

I heard a little squeal from Gwendolyn in the rear of the van. I could tell she was about to shout "Hallelujah!" but had caught it in time.

Nadjina introduced our new guide and then stalked away.

Trying to conceal my delight, I called, "See you later, Nadjina."

She turned with a smirky smile and, as usual, had the last word, "Yes, *much* later."

Now what, I wondered, did she mean by that?

Our local guide was a woman in her early thirties. Her jet black hair was pulled back from a long face accented by piercing eyes set under heavy black brows. She wore a charcoal gray suit with a skirt that hung way below the knees.

Pointing to the walled fortress, she said, "And now we will visit the kremlin."

"Kremlin?" we asked. "Isn't that in Moscow?"

No, she said, the word *kremlin* means fortress. "There are many kremlins in Russia," she continued. "This one in Novgorod is a very ancient one; in fact, the original city was built up around it."

As we walked down the street toward the entrance, we saw a large group of girls about junior-high-school age standing in formation. Dressed in blue skirts with white blouses, each carried a red flag. Parked before them was an official-looking black auto with a loudspeaker mounted on top. From the speaker a metallic voice blared orders to the girls who all dutifully marched in place, waving their flags on command.

As I watched these young teen-agers energetically performing for the state, I was reminded that it is against Communist law to be a member of a church before age twenty-one. It was easy to see which belief got first crack at their young, impressionable minds. We surmised they were rehearsing for tomorrow's May Day festivities. I thought of drum majorettes and marching bands back in the States. I'm sure the others had similar impressions, for suddenly the idea of visiting museums and war memorials palled on us. We were much more interested in these attractive-looking kids, many of whom were watching us curiously.

However, our guide evidently would have none of this nonsense. Answering our questions about the youth group with a short "Yes, they are practicing for tomorrow," she hurried us along into the caverns of the dark and ancient kremlin.

In contrast to Nadjina, our present guide was a fountain of information. Obviously well-educated and intellectual, she enjoyed her work. So much so, that as we continued on past endless display cases of artifacts of Russian history, I noticed some of our group beginning to drift away.

But then we stepped into another roomful of exhibits at which we gasped. Glowing in rich lustrous colors were hundreds of Russian ikons, the famous religious paintings on wood venerated in Russian Orthodox churches. Many of the ikons portrayed various phases in the life of Christ, others the Virgin Mary. As our guide pointed out, Peter and John the Baptist were also popular ikon figures.

All were beautiful and expressive under a glazelike finish that now shone with a patina of centuries. Many dated back to the fifteenth century and some were painted as early as the twelfth century.

Our guide pointed out how various ikons illustrated the history of Novgorod and showed us some portraying defenders of the city carrying the cross into battle. I was impressed by the versimilitude our guide expressed in describing these Christian works. She

spoke with the same knowledgeability of early Christendom as many Bible college professors I knew.

As we walked among lustrous panels of saints lifting their tragic eyes to heaven, the impact of the situation struck me. Our guide was referring to the Christian ikons in the same manner my Bible college professors described ancient Sumerian fertility rites, as if the religion they represented was a fable from the distant past.

We passed through a "library" of beautiful ancient Bibles and many famous theological works that were long out of print. I thought of how many people studying for the ministry in the United States would love to study some of these old books. Yet, every one of them was locked under heavy thick plate glass, obviously never meant to be used by those who placed them here.

As we continued through the somber halls, I remembered Saint Sofia's Cathedral nearby.

"Oh," I said, "we were interested in the cathedral."

"Oh, yes," brightened our guide, pleased at our knowledgability.

We continued out into a courtyard lined with massive sculptures of historic figures including many czars. As she described these I was interested to see that these colorful despots of the past, as ruthless and dictatorial as many were, were still admired today.

What was it, I wondered, that made these old czars understandable to the Communist leaders today, but Christianity an anathema? Could it be that one represented the material so well understood by the State leaders and the other, the spiritual, which is in complete contradiction to the Communist philosophy?

Saint Sofia's loomed before us, its gold dome sparkling against the spring blue sky. Once a church, it is now a museum.

"How long has it been since there was a worship service here?" I asked.

"Before the Revolution," our guide answered with pride.

As we walked through its hushed interior, we heard how the ikons were set up between the worshipers and the altar. It was as if the veil between God and the worshipers was never rent, a symbol, I thought, of how the old official church of Russia maintained a distance between it and the people.

Was this why the official church had ceased to become meaningful in that it had not truly represented the gospel of God's grace and love?

Excitement stirred within me as I thought of the many true Christian believers in Russia today. Would they be the beginnings of a new birth of the Russian people?

As if to challenge this thought, when we finally broke out into the fresh early spring air, huge red banners hanging along the street above us seemed overpowering as they proclaimed: ALL GLORY TO LENIN AND TO THE U.S.S.R.

Viktor was waiting to escort us back to our vans. We waited for the others to assemble, including our own wayward strays who rather sheepishly rejoined us. And then we started walking back to the vans.

Ted was in the rear of the crowd and I walked along with him. Since Viktor was ahead, I felt it safe to ask if anything new had developed on our approval to enter Moscow.

"The same old evasions," he said. "But when we get to Kalinin tonight, we'll see if any new word has come from Moscow. If not, we'll sit down with good old Intourist and settle it once and for all. After all," Ted added emphatically, "our visas are stamped for Moscow. That should be proof enough for *anybody*."

"But what happens if they say no?" I asked.

Ted looked around us, then stepped closer to me and said quietly, "We've got a plan."

We walked along saying nothing for a moment. Life in Novgorod continued around us as usual. Old people walked in the spring sunshine, white swans glided along the shores of a lagoon, and children quietly played on the grass as they do everywhere else in the world. I waited for Ted to continue.

"It was a blessing that Viktor and Nadjina weren't with us in the van this morning," he said. "For we were able to spend all our time in prayer about what to do. My group kept saying that God would lead us. And I finally had to tell them, that wasn't enough. I had to *know* what God wanted us to do."

I looked at Ted as he talked. I could see the tired lines about his eyes. The pressure of leadership was beginning to show its strain.

"So we prayed for a long time as we traveled along, just asking God to show us what to do," he continued.

"And then, one by one, the people began to speak as they were led and our guidance came."

Ted and I stopped for a moment at the rail of a little bridge and looked down at two white swans slowly gliding along the water.

"One girl said that for some time she was given the feeling that if things didn't go exactly as we planned, that we were not to be concerned, that we were just to follow the Lord's leading as the situation developed."

He grinned, "She put it very simply, just 'trust and obey.' And then someone else had the feeling that we should leave the hotel for Moscow tomorrow morning at 4 A.M. And," he added, looking significantly at me, "another said he was given the distinct impression that Viktor and Nadjina would not be with us.

"So," said Ted, exhaling as he leaned down and picked up a branch on the sidewalk, "it boils down to two simple plans: Plan A is that everything will go as normally planned, if we get clearance from Moscow tonight. If not, then it will be Plan B. And that means we'll all quietly get up early in the morning at 4 A.M., slip out of the hotel, and make a run for it."

10

Trapped!

I shuddered at Ted's last statement. Already I was visualizing black sedans full of KGB men pursuing us with guns blazing.

Suddenly I was jolted out of my thoughts by someone shouting in Russian. It was Nadjina. We had reached our vans to find capitalism flourishing in all its glory.

A large group of boys ranging in age from about seven years old to teen-agers had descended on our group. All were armed with May Day souvenirs, badges with hammers and sickles, others emblazoned with "All Glory to the USSR" and some simply saying "Intourist." They were selling them to kids in our group.

A brisk business had started until Nadjina, who obviously didn't want us to have this picture of Russian youth, charged up like an attacking hawk. And like a flock of frightened chickens, the boys scattered into the park. She caught one youngster and confiscated his badge.

She settled next to me in the van, her face set, looking straight ahead. Then, whether it was because she was embarrassed for losing her temper or had become a bit weary of her rigid pose, she turned. "Here," she said, "a trophy," and handed me a badge marked "Intourist." Then she turned back and continued looking straight ahead as we drove through the streets of Novgorod.

"Why, thank you, Nadjina," I said, truly trying to express gratitude more for her change of attitude than the "trophy." I glanced at her out of the corner of my eye as we drove along. She

wasn't much older than myself. Is this what the state does to young people, I wondered, forms them into rigid molds in which they don't really wish to fit?

As we continued through Novgorod we passed a large cemetery. A large number of grave markers in the shape of crosses caught my eye. Did the state leave these as relics of the past, too?

Many people seemed to be visiting the graves to decorate them, just as they do on holidays back in the States. I was struck by the incongruity of it. People decorating Christian graves on a holiday dedicated to atheism.

Was this another clue to what really lived in the hearts of the Russian people?

However, practically all of the churches we passed denied this thought. For all were closed. Some were obviously being used as warehouses or were boarded up, all reminders of the uselessness of Christianity to contemporary Russia. We passed one former church which was quite close enough to the road for us to note the paint peeling off its weather-beaten siding. On its sagging door hung a large padlock.

Would the people's hearts be padlocked to Christ when we started our witnessing in Red Square? I shivered. We'd certainly find out tomorrow.

As we passed more relics of a dead faith, I remembered the Scripture verse one of our group was particularly impressed with at the beginning of our trip. It was from Isaiah, chapter 5. "My beloved had a vineyard on a very fertile hill. He digged it and cleared it of stones, and planted it with choice vines; he built a watchtower in the midst of it, and hewed out a wine vat in it; and he looked for it to yield grapes, but it yielded wild grapes."

It seemed such a strange message at first. But now we began to understand its reference, especially since this chapter goes on to say that this land shall be desolate. Oh, Russia, once a country so full of promise, so destined for greatness under the Lord. What had gone wrong so that now it has produced wild grapes?

We drove up in front of what Nadjina described as a former monastery. A large rectangular stone wall enclosed a cathedral and a number of small buildings in which, Nadjina said, the monks used to live.

Now children played among the buildings, accompanied by a number of dogs which set up a ferocious barking as we approached. We could see scaffolding surrounding many of the buildings. Viktor explained that the monastery was being converted into a motel. "It will be a motel with a historic background," he proudly proclaimed.

As my mind went back to all of the closed churches, I suddenly realized that Christ's church could never be expressed in bricks and mortar, for the material would always be subject to the world, no matter how grandly built.

Christ's church could only be built in people's hearts. But for how long could we keep the Christianity in *our* hearts a secret? It was getting increasingly more difficult.

This fear of exposure constantly rode on our shoulders. And we'd try to joke it off, like today at lunch in Novgorod; one's neighbor would raise a saltshaker or glass of water to your lips as if it were a microphone and say, "Would you mind repeating that please?"

But now in the van as we left Novgorod, I began to feel more confident. We were on our way to Kalinin, our jumping-off place for Moscow. One way or another, we would be leaving tomorrow morning for Red Square. It was only two hours away from Kalinin!

As we rolled along through the countryside we saw the ever-present log cabins. Many of the obviously older ones were leaning in about three directions. New houses were going up and, yes, they were log cabins, too. I wondered why a country that was one of the leaders in space exploration would still use log cabins?

Again, I wanted to ask Nadjina about this but thought better of it. Besides, something interesting was showing up ahead of us on the road. As we approached, we could see it was some kind of small memorial park. In the center of it squatted a huge tank. Our kids had been singing their old high-school songs and as our caravan slowly filed by the memorial, Nadjina turned and silenced us sharply.

"This," she said, "is one of the tanks used by the valiant defenders of Kalinin against the Nazis in World War II. We shall enter Kalinin soon," she continued. "You will find it a very beautiful and interesting city."

She said it was originally called Tver but was renamed in 1933 for "Mikhail Ivanovich Kalinin, a heroic revolutionist and the first president of the Soviet Union."

As our caravan continued to roll along into the dusk we could see spires and onion-topped domes ahead of us. Some of the kids were not really listening to Nadjina as she continued her tour-guide spiel, for the landscape was quite beautiful now with the setting sun casting long shadows across the road.

I sank into my own thoughts, too, thinking how when we reached Kalinin we'd be only eighty miles from Moscow. I looked at my watch—6 P.M. Only six hours until May Day!

As Nadjina continued talking, her voice suddenly lost its flat tour-guide tone and took on a definite edge as if she were issuing an order.

"Tomorrow morning," she stated, "we shall tour Kalinin by special bus. In the afternoon, we shall cruise the Volga River."

After snapping this out as if she were a judge pronouncing sentence, she turned and faced the front of the bus and was quiet. Our minibus suddenly became very quiet. True, we heard rumors about us not being allowed to enter Moscow but we had always shrugged off that possibility with hope. But now to have it stated so officially!

I could hear a few attempts at questions among the group but

the owners quickly swallowed their words. It didn't seem to be the time to ask questions now.

And now I knew we would definitely go through with Plan B in the morning.

As we drove up to our hotel in Kalinin, we all made sure we parked in an open area right by the hotel. After we got out of the buses, Ted checked to make sure that we faced streets that would take us right to the highway leading to Moscow. We wanted to be ready to make our break for Moscow tomorrow, quickly and quietly.

Ted headed straight for the Intourist office to get the final official decision on our entry to Moscow. "When Viktor saw that our visas were in order he said he'd send a Telex to Moscow to straighten out the situation," said Ted. "It could be," he added, as he left, "that everything will work out all right. After all, our official visas should mean something."

We headed into the lobby where, as per our usual practice, we piled all our gear in the middle of the room and slumped down onto chairs, benches, and the floor to wait for our room assignments. I looked around; it was the usual Russian hotel. For some reason all of them we stayed in seemed to be built of concrete. And even though seemingly built recently, the concrete was beginning to crumble. Even the wall tiles in the bathrooms, I noted, were put in crookedly. Could there be crooked contractors in the workers' paradise? I wondered.

It was now 7 P.M. and I was so tired I didn't care if we ate or not. All I could think about was that bed waiting upstairs. Beds were one of the good things I found in Russia. All of their beds seemed to be extra long which was ideal for my six-feet, six-inch frame. Usually in European beds I have to sleep with my feet hanging over the end.

While half dozing, I suddenly heard, "I want all drivers to meet me in the corner of the lobby!" I looked up to see Viktor standing in the center of our group. Next to him stood a man in a light tan trench coat smoking a cigarette.

Tony, Chris, Jim, Ralph, and I struggled to our feet and followed Viktor over to the lobby.

While we walked, the man in the trench coat casually introduced himself as "Andre." He spoke perfect English and was very polite. Neither he nor Viktor ever did say why he was present, but it seemed to be in some official capacity.

Viktor waited for us to gather around him. Then, he made his announcement in firm, clipped words: "It is a rule of this hotel that your vehicles must be parked inside their garage—for their protection."

He looked at each of us intently, and continued: "All of you are to follow Andre and place your vehicles inside the garage *now*."

We drivers looked at each other, careful not to show the consternation that now raged in our hearts.

Plan B had been effectively wiped out.

11

You Can't Fight City Hall

We five drivers stood there, our mouths open. Our vans might as well be locked in the city jail as far as tomorrow morning was concerned. Thoughts stormed my mind. How much *did* they know about us? Had they been listening in on us along the road through some secret sonic device?

At Andre's directions, we drove a hundred yards down the street toward big garages, their doors open, waiting to swallow our vans.

Ralph, driving the Red Square, was first to go in. It had no roof rack and easily slipped through the door opening. But as I approached, I worried about our rack. It would be a tight squeeze. A policeman kept waving me on. As I inched through the door, I heard my rack rubbing. "Stop!" yelled Ralph, who was now standing outside. "You won't make it!"

I backed out. The policeman ordered me back in. Again, that horrible scraping noise. I thought about our van rental contract in which we had to pay $75 for any damage.

"*Nyet, nyet,*" I cried, pointing upwards.

Finally, the policeman was convinced. Now the situation became hilarious. Even though the remaining vans stood as high or higher than mine, the policeman, through some inscrutable logic, insisted that each one try to make it through the door.

Jim, who was next, carried it off well. As soon as his rack

scraped, he leaped out, pointing up and screaming, "Twenty-five rubles! Twenty-five rubles!"

Then it was Chris's turn.

Last in line was the big van, its top rising far above the rest. Yes, it had to be tried, too.

Then the policeman directed us to the other garage—it had taller doors. But when they were opened, the interior was so full of buses that one could have hardly squeezed a bicycle inside.

"Thank You, Lord!"

Andre now ordered us to pull all our vans around the garages into an open courtyard and park there. "They'll be safe," he assured us. "A guard is on duty here all night."

However, we were glad to notice that they faced an open driveway leading to the street. Maybe, just maybe we'd still be able to pull it off. But that would have to wait until 4 A.M. tomorrow!

As we walked out of the courtyard, we noticed Andre in a huddle with the two policemen. As he talked, he kept looking over his shoulder at us and we overheard the word "Moscow" repeated several times.

Back at the hotel we were all ushered into a small private dining room for dinner. To reach it we walked through the large public room in which a band was playing. Many people were dancing and much of the music was very modern American jazz. As we passed the tables, there sat four Christian journalists who were covering our trip. One lifted his finger off his glass in greeting as we passed.

In our little dining room, Viktor and Nadjina were already eating. The rest of us waited as usual until everyone assembled for, even though we didn't say grace openly, this did allow us a quick moment of togetherness in silent prayer.

So far, none at my table knew what success Ted had with Intourist. Jeff mentioned that Ted had heard from some other people who had experience with Intourist that the only technique in which to get your way with them was "to make a big stink about it." Ted had told Jeff that "we just might have to do that."

After all, we had paid to see Moscow. It was stamped on our visas. We had every legal and moral right to go there. In fact, our

visas *ordered* that we "must enter the country on April 29th and proceed to the following destinations: Novgorod, Kalinin, Moscow."

Just as we were finishing our main course of minute steaks, Viktor stood up, tapped on a glass with a spoon, and asked everyone to give him their attention. Again, his voice had that sharp, uncompromising ring.

"I am about to announce our planned schedule for tomorrow," he said, biting each word off like Eric Von Stroheim in an old war movie. "We will have breakfast here in this room at 9 A.M., take Intourist buses for a tour of the city of Kalinin, followed by a boat ride on the Volga River. And," he added on a note of finality, "then we will return to our hotel. Thank you very much." He sat down and continued eating.

There was total silence in the room for a few seconds as the impact of his message sank in, then small gasps and pained exclamations. We all looked at Ted who was sitting at Viktor's table.

Miriam, a girl from the States, and Madeline, from New Zealand, both very sweet and tactful girls, went up to Viktor and asked, "But why? Why can't we go to Moscow?"

Viktor shot up, his jaw muscle tight. "You have been told

many times already," he snapped, his voice rising, "it doesn't *say* 'Moscow' on your tour voucher!"

Now Ted stood up. "That's ridiculous!"

Viktor wheeled to him, "We go to Intourist office *now* and settle this once and for all." They both strode out of the room.

Again, our room was still. Then, suddenly, spontaneously, all fifty of us rose up and in one group followed them. Now most of us were raising our voices as to how ridiculous this was—that we didn't travel all the way across Europe to see Kalinin. We burst into the main dining room. The band stopped playing and everyone's eyes were riveted on us. Out through the lobby and down the hall we marched to the Intourist office. Inside sat Ted, Viktor, Nadjina, an Intourist man, and two Intourist women.

The older Intourist woman pointed to a paper she held. "There is no way we can change this. Your tour itinerary does not have accommodations for Moscow on it."

"But," answered Ted, "we don't want to *sleep* in Moscow; we don't even need a hotel there. We have our rooms here in Kalinin. As I said before," he added patiently, "all we want to do is visit Moscow for the day and return here tomorrow night."

The young Intourist man impatiently smoothed back his black hair. "Only those tourists with accommodations in Moscow can visit the city."

Ted answered quietly, "I don't believe that."

"There is no room for you in Moscow."

"Do you mean to say that in your great capital, there is no room for fifty-one people to stand on the sidewalks?"

No one answered though we could see Andre trying to hold back a chuckle.

"We are here because we love the Russian people," Ted added, "and want to be at the May Day festivities. Can't you approve this?"

"We don't have the authority."

"Who *does* have the authority? Should we call Mr. Brezhnev or Mr. Kosygin?"

Tony stepped in and added very calmly, "You know we're trying to build new relations between your country and mine. In fact, I think some of the bread I was just eating at your table was made with some of the wheat raised in my home state of Nebraska."

His statement seemed to have some effect on the older Intourist woman. She got up and said, "When your itinerary first came to me, I thought it strange that you were not booked to go to Moscow. I called our Moscow office and they said you would not be there."

Ted answered, "Baloney! I have my official itinerary right here and it *was* approved through the booking agency!"

"Then your agency tricked you."

Ted said nothing for a moment. I could see he was trying to control his temper. Then he said slowly and evenly, "Most of us have spent our last bit of money to make this trip and have gone through much hardship to get here. It would be a tragedy if we couldn't see Moscow, the one place we have dreamed of."

Again the words touched hearts. "Well," the older woman said more softly, *"we* can't do anything, especially since the chief of the Kalinin Intourist bureau isn't here."

"Then call him at home."

She hemmed and hawed, then reluctantly picked up the phone.

As we waited for the Intourist chief to arrive, Ted recommended that we get the vans from the garage courtyard, if possible, and pull them up in front of the hotel. Five fellows went out. Fifteen minutes later they were back; they had no trouble. They said the guard just watched them.

Now, we had plenty of work to do and time was flying. A number of kids went up to their rooms and started making preparations for tomorrow. Out came the paper, scissors, and felt pens we'd carefully carried with us, and a regular assembly-line crew started working on our witnessing material.

One group of kids started cutting out the large paper crosses on which they wrote in Russian: JESUS LOVES YOU! and CHRIST IS RISEN! Others worked on large banners proclaiming these messages. And over at the table sat a troop carefully hand-printing leaflets in Russian which included Bible verses and explanatory messages. Greg, Gwendolyn, and Rudy, our Russian linguists, had already printed up models and the others were copying them.

Gwendolyn showed me how the ones she was making fit right under a gum wrapper! Reggie came up from downstairs, "Nick, the Intourist chief is here."

The Intourist chief was an older man who looked very irritated at having to leave his home late at night for some crazy kids. Short and stocky, he looked a little like Brezhnev. He slumped down at his desk, and lighted a cigarette. With him and Andre, the place really became a smoke-filled room.

Ted asked the rest of us to wait in the hall while he continued negotiations. The room was getting hot and we could see that things might go better if the Intourist people felt less pressure.

The hotel staff kept walking by in the hall, nervously looking at us. One cleaning lady took a flower out of a wall container, gave it to Miriam and hugged her. Miriam hugged her back. The lady couldn't speak English and Miriam didn't know a word of Russian. But it was a beautiful case of two hearts understanding each other. Again, I thought of how warm and friendly the average Russian was. Why couldn't the "officials" be the same way?

We could hear Ted's voice rising in the little office as he argued. Finally, he came out into the hall. "Well," he said, wiping his forehead, "we've gotten nowhere with those people. They just keep giving us the same old thing."

He stood quietly for a moment, as if deciding the best way to announce something, then spoke, "So . . . I told them that we were planning to go to Moscow by ourselves by four o'clock this morning."

Everyone gasped, "Wow!" in a kind of affirmative.

"But I have to tell you," added Ted, "that right after I made that statement, Viktor warned me that we shouldn't do it. He said that if we went, 'the consequences would be severe.' "

Ted looked around at each of us. "Is there anyone who doesn't want to go?" There was silence. We were all in unity.

Now we needed our passports. As is usual in Russia, the hotel had collected our passports to keep overnight. But we needed them now. Our 4 A.M. departure was only a few hours away.

"No!" roared the Intourist chief when asked. "You'll get them *when* you leave!"

"Now!" we demanded, knowing that a lot could happen between now and 4 A.M. He ordered us out of his office. Each of us demanded the right to call our embassies. Someone grabbed a phone to get an outside line but it was blocked.

"Nobody is making *any* calls," said Andre. His voice had that steely edge.

"This wouldn't happen in the United States," I said.

"Where anyone can become president?" asked Viktor sarcastically.

Suddenly, everybody was talking and arguing. Then a big husky cleaning lady swooped into the office, said something angrily in Russian, and turned off the lights. It seemed she had been long held up from cleaning this room and this was her way of telling everyone to clear out.

Someone turned the lights back on. But it had broken the tension and everyone was laughing.

Evidently this infuriated the cleaning lady and back in she came, snapping off the lights again. This went on back and forth.

But despite the hilarity, they still wouldn't return our passports. "Please," pleaded Nadjina, "all of you, go now to your rooms. Do what they tell you."

We just sat there, saying nothing.

The Intourist chief buried his head in his hands, then looked up at us with baleful eyes and roared something in Russian. Viktor turned to us, "He said that if you don't leave right now, he'll call the police."

"Go ahead."

In about five minutes a huge burly policeman strode in. He said something in Russian. We sat silently. He repeated it with a note of anger in his voice.

Viktor came to the rescue. "He's saying 'Good evening' and you'd better answer him."

"Good evening!" we all chorused in unison.

"Why are your vehicles not parked where the hotel asked you to put them?" he roared.

The Intourist chief grabbed his arm and in Russian evidently explained that was yesterday's news. He had been called here for another reason.

"I see," said the policeman, regarding each of us. "Well, if you don't go to your rooms right now, I will be forced to take other measures."

"When we have our passports, we will go to our rooms."

"Well," he bellowed, "I'm forced to take other measures." He did a military about-face and strode out of the room, heels clicking.

"Oh, Lord," I prayed, "what's the purpose of all this? Do you want us to go to jail so we can witness *there?*"

The cleaning lady swept back into the room again and angrily turned off the lights.

Perhaps she turned the tide. The Intourist chief wearily lifted his head and beckoned to Viktor. They conferred for a moment, then Viktor turned to us. "Looks like you kids win," he said, "you've got your passports."

Within seconds we were all bunched at the hotel desk, banging on it and yelling, "Passports! Passports!" Out came a harried-looking woman with her hands full of them.

It was now after 1 A.M. and we all headed for our rooms. There was still a lot of work to be done. As I was about to ascend the long wide staircase, I saw a number of men file in the front door. They all wore black suits and black ties. They couldn't be anything but KGB men. The Intourist chief welcomed each of them with a big bear hug, then all moved into the private dining room.

It was clear that there was a top-level KGB meeting going on. And then I chuckled to myself. Out of the room came our old friend from Novgorod, wearing the same trench coat and bright green felt hat. He got a big bear hug from a man at the door and left the hotel.

I went upstairs and watched the cross-makers at work. The room was now festooned with white paper crosses, each with a piece of looped string.

I hung one around my neck. "Think I'll go downstairs like this and walk in on that KGB meeting," I said.

"This is no time for jokes," said Gwendolyn. "Work or get out."

I looked for Ted. Already under heavy pressure, he was understandably wary about sleeping in his room. If he fell asleep, he felt that someone might come in during the night, pull him out and interrogate him, or worse. So we set two lounge chairs in the middle of the hall and sat looking at each other. Ted said some of the kids were staying in the vans.

"All that someone need do," he said, "is pour some of that thick Russian syrup in the gas tanks and that would be the end of Moscow for us."

As we talked we saw the young Intourist man peek up over the top of the stairs. Then the older woman from his office came up, clicked past us, head held high, and stopped to knock at a door down the hall. She knocked for several minutes. But no answer. She clicked back and went downstairs.

"What was *that* all about?" wondered Ted.

Five minutes later, Viktor walked out of that door, still wearing his black suit and black turtleneck sweater.

As he passed, he looked at us in surprise: "You guys still up?"

"Yeah," said Ted, "we'll never get out of here by four if we go to sleep now."

Viktor stopped, his face softened, and he gave a low laugh, "You guys are something else."

Ted sat up. "Hey Vik, ol' buddy. We don't know the way. Was it that road that we were on before we turned off to Kalinin?"

Viktor hesitated for a second, looked over his shoulder, then smiled, "Yeah, that's the road."

"Thanks," said Ted.

"Don't mention it," said Viktor. He shrugged his shoulders and went downstairs to what we presumed was the security men meeting.

We continued talking, trying to stay awake. Then Ted said quietly, "Nick, let's pray for a while." And so we did. It was a beautiful time of fellowship with the Lord. We talked to Him about the trip and asked for His protection.

Ted and I continued talking about what the Lord wanted us to do in Moscow. Every once in a while his eyes would close. I'd stop talking and he'd nod for about a minute, then bob awake to continue his conversation right where he left off.

As we talked, I could hear muffled noises from the rooms where many kids were still at work on the crosses, banners, and tracts.

I looked at my watch—3:30 A.M. It was time to get everybody together. It was time to go to Moscow.

12

Moment of Truth

The girls looked beautiful, absolutely beautiful. It was 3:45 A.M. and our group had begun to quietly gather in the hall. The old jeans, slacks, and dungarees had been left behind and, in honor of the occasion, the girls had donned long skirts and dresses. Many had done up their hair.

"Wow! I didn't know we had *girls* on this tour!"

"Well, *some* of you fellows look pretty nice, too," hissed Sheena, pointedly looking at the few guys who wore suit coats and ties. Unfortunately, the rest of us couldn't do much with our limited wardrobes.

It was eerily quiet in the hall. Only the creaking of the old wood floor indicated activity. Stragglers drifted in from their rooms, rubbing sleepy eyes. We assembled in an air of hushed expectancy as does a graduating class gathering for the grand march. For we knew that no matter what happened, today would undoubtedly prove to be one of the most unusual days in our lives.

Finally, everyone was accounted for. Ted stood before us for a long moment, looking at us, unspoken love flowing between us. We silently prayed, then looked up.

"Okay," he whispered, "let's go."

We silently stole down the long, wide staircase, stepped into the still lobby. As we passed through it, we saw a number of policemen snoring in the chairs. Not all were fully asleep, however. For after we passed, some of them got up and went to the phones.

We stepped out into the black street. A faint gray light washed the eastern horizon and a brisk cold wind swept down the empty street. It carried the frigid bite of the Arctic. Had it come all the way from Siberia? I wondered.

It was now 4 A.M. in Kalinin. Halfway around the world in New Jersey, it was 8 o'clock in the evening. Mrs. Peter Ottalagano was getting ready to close her family's dry-cleaning shop. As she reached for her keys, she suddenly felt a deep burden for Nick Savoca, the young man who had married her pastor's daughter. She had met him recently and knew only that he was on a special mission somewhere in Russia, something that had to do with May Day. She sat down by the steam presser, bowed her head and started to silently pray for him. At this moment, her 19-year-old son came in from a delivery. "Say, Mom," he called, "have you heard anything about that guy who married Rozanne?"

Mrs. Ottalagano looked up through tear-filled eyes. "How is it," she asked, "that you, too, think of him at this moment?"

"Mom, I just had a strong feeling in my heart for him."

The two sank to their knees and together prayed for Nick Savoca and all the young people with him.

In England, New Zealand, Scotland, Ireland, Australia, South Africa, and Finland, similar scenes took place as people prayed for the little crusade. In many churches parishioners began fasts and prayers that would continue through May Day.

On the dark street in front of the hotel, our vans waited for us. I turned the key; our engine coughed, spit, and finally started. I winced, afraid we would awake the entire hotel. Now all engines were humming. Slowly Ted pulled away, and we followed. We were off to Moscow!

We headed out of Kalinin and soon saw the silhouette of the tank memorial against the dawn sky at the crossroads. To the left was Moscow, 100 miles east. We swung onto the highway and accelerated. Soon we were bouncing over the familiar potholes and our spirits soared. We had gotten away! We gave thanks to God for we felt like the Red Sea had parted before us.

Everyone in our bus became very quiet. We were still apprehensive and each of us in his own way was praying to reach our destination, and for protection. Then, in a burst of exuberance, Sheena threw up her arms in praise and her elbow jabbed me in the eye.

"Ouch, praise the Lord!" I shouted.

"Oh, Nick, I'm so s-o-r-r-y!"

"Okay," I laughed, "but you're more dangerous than the KGB."

Soon we spotted the first highway checkpoint where drivers must show their credentials. We held our breaths, slowed, but the guardhouse was dark. We cheered and accelerated. They hadn't gotten up early enough for us!

Now we were only eighty miles from Moscow. We should be in Red Square in two hours!

An old-fashioned revival was now threatening to split the sides of our minibus! But, above the singing, I heard a familiar thumping on our roof. I knew the sound too well. It was our tarp working loose. I pulled over and the caravan came to a halt to wait while I got out and secured it.

As I secured the tarp, the kids inside the van continued singing. Suddenly, they stopped. I looked down the highway. Until now we had not met a single vehicle.

A black sedan approached. I watched as I pretended to tie the tarp. The car moved past us about twenty-five miles per hour. Inside sat two men wearing black hats and coats, the same type of men we saw gathering in the hotel lobby last night.

The sedan disappeared up the road behind us. Then, as I was getting back in the van, it came back again, moved slowly past us, then accelerated and was soon lost in the distance.

"Who do you think they were?" asked Rudy.

I had my suspicions, but didn't want to say.

"Oh, c'mon," laughed Gwendolyn, "let's not get so ap-pre-hen-sive!"

"Yeah," added Greg, "let's get this show on the road. I don't want to miss the parade."

Now, prayerfully apprehensive, we sped along. Soon we

reached a flat plains area. The land seemed marshy. Silhouetted against the far horizon were low bulks of distant factories.

"In another seventy miles we'll be in Red Square," called Jill, "better start practicing our *Christos voskresen.*"

"*Christos voskresen!* Jesus loves you!" we began to chant. "*Christos voskresen!*"

The chant caught in our throats.

Far down the highway sat a giant truck-trailer parked directly across it. One lane was open but blocking it was the black sedan we had just seen. Beside the highway loomed a checkpoint tower.

Even from here we could see the police van at its base and the armed figures standing around it.

It was a full-fledged roadblock.

I knew it was ridiculous but I frantically searched for escape routes leading off the highway. But the highway led us relentlessly to the roadblock.

As we approached, a policeman headed for Ted's van. With a black-and-white-striped wand he waved Ted back. "Turn around," he called, "go back, go back."

Ted continued moving ahead, then stopped beside the policeman. He was a smooth-faced boy, no older than eighteen. His face mirrored apprehension mixed with resolve as he strode up to Ted's window.

Ted leaned out and handed him his visa. We could see Ted point and hear him say, "Approved for Moscow."

Now confusion clouded the policeman's face. He hesitated, then waved our caravan on to an older policeman who was obviously his superior.

We almost laughed in recognition. It was the same burly officer who had told us in the Intourist office last night that he was going to "take other measures."

Was this the "other measure?"

Ted again leaned out profferring his visa. The man just kept shaking his head. "Go back! Go back!" he shouted, waving.

Now our caravan had halted. Through my open window I could hear a low murmur coming from the vans. Just as in our van, everyone was storming heaven with prayer.

We sat looking at the police, at the truck-trailer, the black sedan. At this moment I believed that a miracle would happen, that the truck would suddenly pull away, or even disappear in thin air. Other kids were praying that the police would receive a phone call from officials in Moscow telling them to let us go through.

For fifteen minutes we sat there praying. Meanwhile the police stood resolute.

Brakes squealed behind us and we looked out to see another sedan drive up. The door swung open and out stepped Andre, our old acquaintance from Kalinin.

He stood on the highway casting a long shadow behind him from the new sun. He lit a cigarette, drew on it, and exhaled the smoke slowly as he looked at us.

Ted opened the door of his van and stepped out. I followed along with Tony, Ralph, and a few other kids. We walked up to Andre.

He dropped his cigarette on the pavement, ground it with his heel. "I suppose by now you are very sick of me," he said wearily, "but I have come here to tell you that you must go back, that you will not be allowed to go to Moscow."

He pointed to the burly policeman. "This man is chief of traffic police. He has orders that you are to return to your hotel in Kalinin immediately."

Ted handed Andre his visa. Andre shrank from it. "I am well acquainted with your visa, thank you," he said. "But it is not enough. I'm sorry. You are not supposed to go to Moscow, and so you will not go to Moscow. We invite you," he continued, "we invite you to go back to your hotel."

We said nothing, frustration mounting within us, knowing that Moscow was only one-and-one-half hours down the highway. To be blocked this close to our goal after all our effort and prayer seemed incomprehensible.

We stood looking at Andre. We could see anger seething just below the surface of his face. He was struggling to control his temper. A chill wind that had increased with the sunrise, whipped his coat around him.

"Look," he continued, "none of you got much sleep last night. Why not go back to your hotel, get some sleep and forget all this?"

Meanwhile traffic was beginning to pick up on the highway. The black sedan shuttled back and forth across the single-lane opening in front of the truck-trailer to allow the traffic to pass through.

I checked my watch—it was nearly 7 A.M., almost two hours since we had been halted by the roadblock. We were now surrounded by some thirty police and KGB men. I looked around; it was a strange little scene. The kids in the vans were quietly watching our little group as we stood in confrontation with Russian power.

I looked at Ted. I could see he was weighing something in his mind, as if he were struggling to come to a decision. I knew he was praying and seeking guidance. His answer wasn't long in coming.

Ted turned to the kids in the vans. "All right," he announced, loud and clear. "We are not going to be allowed to go farther than here." He waited a moment, then continued, "I have the guidance," he stated, "that we should preach the gospel of Jesus Christ to these people right here and now!"

An electrifying thrill shot through me. And a unanimous roar of approval, "Praise God!" resounded from the vans.

We could be Christians openly again!

Everyone tumbled out of the vans carrying their large paper crosses. Many held them high in the air as if they were flaming torches, others put them around their necks. And then, all fifty-one of us standing together, raised our hands to heaven, looked up and began singing lustily: "Hallelujah, for the Lord our God, the Almighty reigns. . . ."

Andre watched us open-mouthed. He quickly turned, walked a short distance away, and lit a cigarette.

As our group stood there beside the highway deep in Russia, it felt so good to be a professing Christian. We continued singing, and chanting: "Christ is risen!" and "Jesus loves you!" in Russian.

More police cars had arrived and now a large number of guards and security men stood before us. In our limited Russian, we told them that we had nothing against them. "We love you . . . we love you," we called.

Some stared sardonically, a few snickered, many smiled bashfully. To one policewoman, however, we were just another part of her work. Armed with an imposing camera, she strode up to us as we were standing in line singing and snapped a closeup, head-and-shoulders portrait of each of us.

Now the traffic passing through the roadblock had become heavy, much of it evidently heading for Moscow.

As cars, trucks, and buses approached, each was forced to stop. And, at each vehicle we waved and held up our crosses. Yesterday we had seen padlocked churches. Today we saw that hearts can never be locked. For we began to get a glimmer of how many Christians there are in Russia today.

As one huge bus groaned by, we held our crosses aloft and waved. Many people at the windows broke out in wide grins and waved back. One beautiful teen-aged girl jumped up from her seat, pressed her radiant face against the window, pointed to her heart, and nodded vigorously.

Truck drivers, motorists, and people riding in the backs of trucks acknowledged us. Some, with one eye on the police, gave us a tentative wave. Others would unashamedly point to heaven, then to their hearts, and nod knowingly.

The anxious police now tried to hurry traffic through the roadblock. But their efforts were of little use. It turned out to be just the same as in our country when something unusual happens alongside the road. Traffic slowed down until a line backed up. Every driver was curious to see what the commotion was.

As more police cars arrived and emptied, we called out, "Praise God, our congregation is growing! We want all of you to know that Jesus Christ is alive and that He loves you!"

Some of our group began to witness to the men individually.

The sky had become overcast and now it began to rain.

"Wow!" exclaimed Tony, "the government even controls the weather here." However, we stayed where we were and continued to sing. The harder it rained, the more we rejoiced. We were not aware of the wet or chill but exulted in worshiping the Lord.

By now we had made up a special chorus in Russian, probably the only Russian words in which we were really fluent: "Christ is risen, risen, risen . . . Oh, Jesus loves you, loves you, loves you . . ."

As we sang my heart swelled. "Oh, God," I prayed, "what a privilege You have given us to come to the middle of Russia and worship You *here.*"

At the same time I felt a warm flood of compassion for my brothers and sisters in Christ who couldn't gather and spontaneously worship as we were doing. I also thought of the Jewish believers who were in bondage.

Andre had since returned to our group and I turned to him. "Andre," I asked, "why does your government persecute the Christians so?"

"Persecute them?" he snapped. "That's what *you* say," he added, flicking away his cigarette butt.

"But we have reports," said Tony.

"False," snorted Andre, "propaganda from troublemakers."

"Then, what is *this?*" I handed him a list of names of Russian Christians now serving prison sentences for their belief. One of our group had smuggled it in with them under a shoe innersole.

Andre studied the list, saying nothing. One of the policemen took it, looked at it, then passed it to another. I saw one point to one of the names on the sheet and nod to his partner as if he were acquainted with the prisoner.

Andre adroitly changed the subject. "We thought all you kids in America had turned off religion."

"Not *all* of us," I grinned.

"I can *see* that," he answered wryly.

A large number of police, plainclothesmen, and guards were now gathered at the checkpoint. And one thing was evident in their faces. They seemed to have a real fear of us. It was not the kind of fear as if we were armed with guns and bombs, but a fear of something they could not understand. Two motorcycle policemen roared up and stopped in front of us. They watched us with interest. Ben, who knew some Russian, went over and began to talk to them. They started to reply until their senior officer stepped over and spoke sharply. They turned their heads from us and sat rigidly on their cycles.

One of the motorcyclists was given orders to go somewhere and as he was stamping his kick starter, one of our people slipped up and stuck a cross on the cycle's rain-slick back fender. The driver roared off, unwittingly displaying a large white cross proclaiming "Christ Is Risen!" The senior officer shouted at him. The cyclist skidded to a stop, looked at his back fender, and in an obvious effort to impress his superior, ripped off the cross and proceeded to tear it in little pieces.

He leaped back on his motorcycle and was about to accelerate away when the officer shouted at him again. This time the man dismounted and shamefacedly proceeded to pick up all the pieces of paper he had scattered on the ground. He looked about for a moment as if searching for a trash container, then impatiently thrust the scraps in his pocket, leaped on his cycle, and roared away.

The Russian government is very careful that its citizens do not litter.

At this Ted held up his hand. "Whoever did that," he said seriously, "should not do it again. That was a trick and we want to be fair and open about our witnessing."

The traffic continued to grind slowly by, each vehicle a front-row audience to our witnessing. Then another car drove up from the direction of Kalinin and out stepped Viktor. We called to him as he walked to the tower. He waved, then ascended to the top of the checkpoint where we could see him at the giant glass windows, looking down at us with that enigmatic smile. Behind him milled a roomful of high officials who seemed to be constantly talking, gesticulating, and making phone calls.

Two hours had now passed since we started our witnessing and some of us began to drift back to our vans to take catnaps. Our sleepless night was telling on us.

Ted and we leaders started discussing what we should do. One of the fellows felt that we should still try and go on to Moscow. The rest of us felt deeply that the Lord had already given us our victory right here. Though we had been stopped from reaching our worldly destination by Soviet power, we had reached the destination that God had set for us.

The Lord was still in charge. The important thing, we felt, was that we had obeyed Him as far as we were able.

Now our inner guidance told us that we had witnessed here as long as He wanted us to. It was now time to head back to Kalinin.

We climbed into the vans, started them up, and tried to turn around. But we couldn't. We were completely hemmed in by police cars, vans, and trucks.

Obviously, we were all under arrest.

13

Now It Can Be Told

It was a scene out of an old Keystone Kops movie. Carloads of police and Party members were still arriving, officials argued and waved their arms, and the tower phones kept ringing incessantly.

The irony of it was that we, who seemed to be the cause of the furor, now wanted to leave but couldn't. All of us were dead tired and many were already draped over the van seats, sound asleep.

Ted and a few of us went up to Viktor who seemed to be the only one at ease. He had come down from the tower and was now leaning against it, his arms folded.

We told him that we felt we had done all we could—all we wanted now was to go back to our hotel.

"We're bushed," I pleaded, "won't they let us go?"

Viktor smiled, "You kids asked for it. I warned you, remember?" He looked up to the tower, his voice softened. "Well, let me see what I can do."

He headed into the maelstrom of guards and police and we went back to our vans. An hour went by. Finally, Viktor came toward us. He stopped at Ted's van, then mine. "You can go back now," he said. "You should feel honored—you'll be escorted by some of our country's finest police." He grinned, "Just like when Brezhnev travels."

Finally, with much waving of police batons and shouts of directions, our little caravan wound around on the highway and headed back to Kalinin. A police car led the way and a large security van followed at our heels. It was a quiet group that drove back up the highway which we had traveled so joyfully this morning. We gave thanks in prayer for having been able to do what had to be done, and also asked guidance to face what was to come.

We soon saw a harbinger of what was to come. At each side road, a police car was stationed. "Just in case we get any funny ideas," mused Rudy. At the now familiar tank memorial, a baton-waving guard was on duty to make sure our entourage turned to Kalinin.

As we drove along, the van became even quieter as the kids drifted off to sleep. I found myself thinking of the roadblock, and self-condemnation crept in. Satan dug at me with, "Certainly, you could have figured *some way* to get past that checkpoint; you were so close to Moscow. Better face it. You all blew it."

I voiced my feelings to Rudy and he admitted to having the same thoughts. Together, in prayer, we turned the whole thing over to the Lord. Back came a wonderful sense of assurance that we had fully done what He wanted.

It turned out that a lot of other kids had been bothered by the same negative feelings. It helped them to hear of our assurance.

By the time our police-led caravan pulled up in front of our hotel, everyone was in high spirits.

It was now 11 A.M. It had been only seven hours since we left the hotel this morning, but it seemed like a month ago.

As we got out of the vans, we got a new surprise. "Look at that!" gasped Sheena, pointing to a line of uniformed figures. The hotel was completely encircled by a police guard. We counted forty-eight formidable-looking men. A cold chill went up my spine. But no one removed their large white paper crosses as they marched bravely into the lobby which was now crowded with people.

A number of Hungarian tourists had arrived that morning.

They were intrigued by our crosses and those who could speak English began to question us about them. We began to share what the Lord had done for us.

Other people stared at our crosses. And we took every opportunity to speak to them. A few shied away from us, looking around with fear in their eyes. But I'll never forget the one man who, with his wife, was just leaving as we walked in. He seemed so impressed with our crosses, that he wheeled about, followed us inside, and came up to whisper, *"Christos voskresen."* His wife hung behind with a worried look. Finally, she came up, took him by the arm, and pulled him out the door. A minute later he had slipped in again with that big smile and another *"Christos voskresen."*

An air of geniality blossomed through the lobby. Jill, feeling it, took out her guitar and we all gathered around her, singing gospel choruses for the pure joy of being in His Spirit.

Viktor came out and held up his hand. Was he going to stop us from singing? "If you can leave your singing for a while," he announced, "the hotel wants you to know they have a brunch set up for you.

"You know," he added, "you all left before breakfast this morning."

There was loud applause from us. We had expected to be treated like villains and, in fact, were expecting word any minute that we must leave the country immediately.

As we walked into the little dining room, still wearing our crosses, Nadjina met us at the door.

"Oh, boy," she laughed, "I usually bring my camera on these tours and, my, do I miss having it today."

"It sounds," she added, "as if you people really put on a show this morning."

"Yes, you really missed it, Nadjina," I said, "I've been wanting to tell you for a long time how much the Lord loves you."

She flushed, turning away. "Yes, yes," she said.

Back in our familiar dining room everyone was in joyful spirits, talking and laughing. Ted got up and rapped on a glass. "We're going to ask the Lord to bless this food."

"Yeah! Amen!" was the resounding chorus.

He turned, "Nick, will you lead us in prayer?"

What a wonderful feeling; it had been so long since we could say grace openly. I raised my hands to heaven. "Oh Lord, we thank You; we thank You for the wonderful time You have given us on this trip, for allowing us to witness to those You love. We thank You for our guides, Nadjina and Viktor, for the kindness of those who gave us this meal, and for all that has happened. We praise You, Lord!"

Everyone joined in with an enthusiastic "Amen!" and the joyful mood continued through our meal.

Then Viktor stood up. The room quieted down. We expected one of his familiar speeches.

"We would like you to know," he said in his this-is-what-you-will-do tone, "that we will still tour Kalinin this afternoon starting at 2 P.M. We will go on buses through the city, and then we will take a boat ride on the Volga."

There were answers of "Hurray! Wonderful! Praise the Lord!" Everybody was feeling good. But I had to chuckle to myself. In typical Slavic thoroughness, we had to take this excursion because our tour voucher "so specified."

After brunch, we went back to the lobby to wait for our tour buses. Chris met a Russian Communist who spoke German. And since Chris was fluent in German, they had quite a conversation. The man wouldn't believe that his country was holding Christians prisoners because of their faith. Chris showed him our list of names. The Communist carefully copied the list. "I'll check into it," he promised.

It was communication like this that gave us an insight into the Russian mind. Communism as a political and economic system seemed to be generally well accepted by the average Russian.

Certainly, the Russians have benefited in a material way. It is the official stand for atheism that seems to be the chink in the Party's armor. For the Russian people seem to have a deep abiding feeling for religion which does not die easily. We could see this in people everywhere.

For example, the same maid who had given Miriam the big hug and flowers last night, came to us in the hall this afternoon with a big smile, nodding her head and pointing to her heart saying, *"Christos voskresen."*

Gwendolyn met three cleaning women in the hotel who "hugged and kissed me at the foot of the stairs. Another crossed herself. It was thrilling!"

As we waited in the lobby, Chris spotted a grand piano and couldn't resist sitting down at it. We all gathered around and soon we were all in the spirit singing gospel songs. For twenty minutes we sang soft and sweet choruses. Some of the kids had their hands raised.

Soon a large crowd of people gathered, including the kitchen staff who came out to listen. Viktor stood by, too. Whether he was intrigued by the music or just the sight of all of us singing, he seemed to enjoy it.

However, the geniality stopped just outside the hotel entrance. Jeff and I had stepped out to see if the buses had arrived and noticed a large crowd of people standing across the street.

"Let's go and tell them about the Lord," said Jeff.

We walked down the steps and started to go past the police. The guard's face was impassive, but his hand wasn't. He planted two fingers in my chest and pushed. I was surprised by the power in those two fingers. "Please don't do that," I said and again tried to pass him. Again, I was forced back. Evidently, Andre had been watching because he came out of the hotel entrance and stepped up to us. "Don't cause trouble," he warned. "We invite you to go back into the hotel."

The iron fist was beginning to show through the velvet glove.

"Are we all under arrest?" I asked. "If we are, then tell us the charges so I can let my embassy know."

Andre didn't answer. By this time plainclothesmen had gone across the street and were now herding the people down the block.

"Well, at least we can call *Christos voskresen* to them," said Jeff. And so we did for the next ten minutes. Others of our group joined us and some witnessed to the KGB men. "Christ is risen," said Bill, one of the Christian journalists. "Nyet Christ," answered the hard-faced KGB man, "Lenin!"

"Ah," answered Bill, "but Lenin's dead." There was no reply. Finally we retreated back into the lobby to find a phenomenon going on. People from all over Kalinin had started coming to the hotel. News that a group of young Christians was at the hotel had spread around the city like wildfire. What was almost as surprising was that the police didn't stop anybody from entering the hotel nor did they even question them. Perhaps it was because they slipped in almost unobtrusively, and they endeavored to remain unobtrusive for it was in the halls and more secluded areas that they would slip up saying, *"Christos voskresen."* However, many of them seemed expectant of something. We couldn't figure it out until a man in work clothes sidled up to Jeff and whispered, "You have Bible?"

So that was it. Sadly, this was a gift that we didn't have to give. However, it did give us the idea to write our own "tracts." We didn't have Bibles but we could give out Scripture. We had a whispered conference and a number of kids dashed up to their rooms and went to work. Some folded up small pieces of paper. The others, with the help of our Russian linguists, Rudy, Gwendolyn, and Alan, started writing out Bible verses on them in Russian. We used John 3:16 and other messages about God's love and salvation.

By now we had determined to make our upcoming bus tour a real witnessing campaign for Jesus. But how far would the police and the KGB let us go?

We "Wowed" Them in Kalinin

As we filed onto the big Intourist buses, we were not ordered to remove our crosses though Nadjina said that "since the people wouldn't understand, you might as well take them off."

The crosses stayed with us and as the buses lumbered through the police lines, they were promptly displayed at the windows.

A local guide was posted on our bus and someone asked her how many churches there were in Kalinin.

"Active ones?" she asked.

"Yes."

"There is one, the Russian Orthodox Church," she said, "but not many attend. Just a few old ladies."

"Isn't that because anybody else attending would be persecuted?" asked Jeff.

The guide just smiled and began a droning commentary on the history of Kalinin. By now we were moving down a busy thoroughfare along which hung vast forty-foot-high portraits of Lenin, Marx, and Engels. It was also crowded with May Day celebrants and instead of listening to the guide, all of us began waving to the people on the street and calling out "Christ is risen" and "Jesus loves you!" Again, many of the people returned our waves and pointed to their hearts.

One middle-aged man in work clothes got so excited that he ran alongside our bus indicating that he was a Christian, too.

Only a few people didn't respond. As we pulled alongside a

124

large trolleybus, I waved to one glum-looking man at the window and lifted my cross. In an unmistakable gesture, he motioned for me to take the string from my cross and hang myself.

"Well," laughed Jeff, "you can't win them all!"

As we moved deeper into Kalinin we passed throngs listening to blaring loudspeakers broadcasting speeches from Red Square.

"Jesus loves you! Jesus loves you!" we called out the windows.

Now our bus turned and started going down an incline. Out the window I saw a river sparkling in the afternoon sun. The Volga! I had to admit I felt a thrill on seeing what I had long heard about in song and story. Of course, some of the kids started singing "The Volga Boatman," and this is the only time our guide seemed to approve of what we were doing.

A crowd of people was standing at the boat dock and we began handing out our tracts. However, the police escorting us rushed over, ripped the tracts from their hands, and began hurrying us to the boat.

"Whuf," gasped Jeff, "instead of a sightseeing tour, I feel like we're being herded into a concentration camp."

I stayed with James, the former monk, who couldn't walk very fast. Together we held our crosses very high. Suddenly, two news cameramen were taking movies of us. We began shouting *"Christos voskresen!"* and held our crosses even higher.

Meanwhile, the people who were ordered to move on had stopped some distance away and stood watching us. Their eyes were very bright.

The excursion boat was quite nice. Freshly painted white, it was about sixty feet long and had seats all the way around, much like our typical sightseeing boats in America. The nicest thing about it was that most of the police stayed on shore. I guess they figured we couldn't get in trouble out on the Volga.

As we moved along at a good clip, a feeling of festivity spread among us and soon we were all talking and laughing. As we passed under a bridge on which some people were standing, we called and held up our crosses. They waved down at us, smiling, and we soon forgot the police.

Our hour's ride was soon over and as we headed for the dock, we could see a large crowd of people waiting. "Look," said Jeff, "I don't see any police. Maybe their schedules are mixed up." It turned out they were all relaxing at a nearby pub.

On getting off the boat, we made the most of our freedom. One man came up to me leading a small boy who looked to be about seven years old. He stopped, looked around fearfully, then motioning to me seemed to ask, "Will you tell my son about Jesus?"

My heart cried out for the two of them. I was so frustrated. If I could have spoken Russian, I would have preached them a sermon. But all I could do was kneel down to the tyke who looked at me with wide, trusting Slavic eyes, and say, "Jesus loves you." One of the girls handed the boy's father some tracts.

As we moved on, I looked back. There stood the father and son, eyes shining, waving to us. Suddenly, they looked around in fright; the father grabbed his son and disappeared in the crowd. We looked beyond the people and saw the police arriving.

We got back to the hotel to find it still under tight guard. But no one needed to worry—all of us were too exhausted that evening to do anything but fall into our beds and sleep the night through. Some of us felt sorry for all those policemen standing out there all night in the cold and wondered if we shouldn't tell their chief that we weren't planning anything.

Wednesday morning, May 2nd, found the Russian people streaming back to their jobs in offices, stores, and factories. Meanwhile, we were packing our vans for the long ride home. We planned to make Novgorod tonight.

All fifty-one of us stood together in a big circle out in front of the hotel, had prayer, and sang our theme song: "Hallelujah, For the Lord Our God the Almighty Reigns." The hotel staff, guests, and even some off-duty police, came out to see us off.

Our biggest surprise came when some of us went into the hotel for the last suitcases. The older Intourist woman who had gotten very angry with us the night before, slipped up and whispered, "As far as I'm concerned, I'd like to have you people come back. We *need* people like you around here."

The police did not share her opinion. In fact, to make sure

that we were well started on our way, a police car escorted us from the rear and another led the way.

This gave Ted an idea. He would drive the last van ahead of the police car. By slowing down, he'd keep the police car behind him and allow the other vans to move further ahead, giving us an opportunity to witness to people in the towns and villages.

We pulled away from Kalinin waving good-byes to all the people in front of the hotel. The policemen watched impassively until we shouted, "Jesus loves you! We love you!" in Russian. Some smiled embarrassedly, others looked at their feet in the front of this warm assault.

Soon we were back in the Russian countryside. The early sun was behind us and our vans cast long shadows down the highway. Down the road we saw a cluster of log cabins. We looked back. Ted and the police car were about a half-mile behind us.

Good! We stopped, got out, and taped our white crosses all over our vans. Up went the banners along the side: JESUS LOVES YOU! and CHRIST IS RISEN!

At each village, we were able to slow to a crawl and call out our greetings. Always, the response was the same, with many people pointing to the sky, then their hearts.

One woman, working in her garden, dropped her hoe and came running to the street. A man snoozing on a bench beside his house, hearing our shouted greetings, jumped up and ran alongside our slow-moving vans calling out in joy.

Our handwritten tracts would flutter to the feet of the villagers as we passed by. They would pick them up, read them quickly, and wave. And now we learned why the Lord led us to take chewing gum on this trip. We would slip tracts inside the wrappers of the sticks. Tossed out to the children, they would be snatched up almost before they reached the ground. As the youngsters scrambled for the gum, I couldn't help but think of Jesus' words in John 4:32: "I have food to eat of which you do not know." Would they ever be given the opportunity to really feast on His words? I wondered.

The way that opportunity would often be blocked was illustrated when we stopped for gas. On seeing our crosses and hearing our greetings, a crowd gathered. By this time, several police cars had begun escorting us, seemingly determined to stick very close to us. As we handed out the tracts at the gas station, the police would rip them out of the people's hands, and tear them up.

But I saw one exception. I noticed a policeman grab a tract from a villager, look to see if his superior was watching, then stuff it into his own pocket. I silently wished him good reading.

As we were going through our usual process of refueling, a bus filled with teen-agers pulled up. They were members of the Communist Youth League. Jeff, wearing cross and all, took a handful of tracts, quickly slipped into the bus, and walked down the aisle handing them out. When he stepped back out a look of complete astonishment covered his face. "I can't believe it," he said, "everyone took one with a smile and they began *reading* them!" We wondered if their open attitude resulted from their being away from the supervision of "the system."

But it wasn't always so easy. When we started up, the police car rode Ted's rear bumper forcing him to keep close to us. When we slowed to drop tracts at another village, the police car screeched up and those who had picked up tracts quickly dropped them.

Sometimes, however, as we would look back to watch our tracts flutter in front of people, they would stand there pretending not to notice the leaflets. Then, as soon as the police car would flash by, they would quickly stoop and pick them up.

But the most hilarious thing happened as we crawled through the towns. In an effort to drown out our greetings, the police would shout over their loudspeakers, "Do not look at these people! Do not listen to them! They are dangerous!" And, of course, just the opposite happened. *Everybody* craned their necks and pushed through roadside crowds to see who these "dangerous" people were.

My most poignant memory is of the old man who had picked up one of the tracts. One of the police cars sped over to him, tires shrieking, and shouted something over the loudspeaker. Startled, the poor old fellow, face frozen with fear, went over to the police and obviously explained that he had no intention of reading the leaflet. He then carried it back to our bus with a quick "I'm sorry, that's the way it is" look on his face, and then looked back toward the police car to make sure that they had seen what he had done. It saddened me to see how fear haunted this man's life.

By now it was time to stop for lunch. But it would be only a roadside respite. Our hotel in Kalinin had thoughtfully made up a bag lunch for each of us. It contained a sandwich, two hardboiled eggs, and a drink.

It was pleasant sitting on the grass at the side of the highway. As we were finishing our sandwiches, Ted stood up and said he had something to tell us. "I realize that all of us are caught up in the excitement of the moment," he said. "But I feel that some of us who are yelling *Christos voskresen* are losing some of the love in our motivation along the way. I fear we are doing it for the wrong reason—for the thrill of defying authority, rather than praising the Lord in love."

All was quiet as Ted stood there, the wind billowing gentle waves in the golden wheat fields behind him. Each one of us, I'm certain, searched his own heart in view of Ted's words.

Those words had cut deeply and it was a shock to have to admit to myself that, more often than not, I was doing it to defy the police.

Ted continued, "Let's remember our motive. If we are not calling out our greetings in honest love, then don't do it at all."

Sitting next to me, Viktor and Nadjina were listening intently. I believe now that Ted's little speech was one of the greatest witnesses for Christian fair play that they could have been exposed to.

We were all deeply impressed, of course. And, after we started up our caravan, I drove quietly for a while. Finally, after some struggle, I asked the others in the van to forgive me for calling out more in defiance than in love. Some admitted that they had been doing it, too.

As the sun began to sink to the western horizon, the onion domes of Novgorod's cathedrals could be seen across the broad plains. Soon we were back in familiar streets. We now felt a greater anointing upon us because we had looked into our own hearts and had asked the Lord to fill us with His love. Our spirits were lifted and again we called out the windows of our van, not in raucous demonstration but in heart-filled greetings. And the response was in kind—hand waves, smiles, and nods.

We continued winding our way through the narrow streets until we were back in front of a hotel in the center of Novgorod. We got out of the vans, assembled together, and spontaneously started singing: "Hallelujah, For the Lord Our God the Almighty Reigns."

As we sang, we noticed a crowd beginning to gather on the sidewalk near us. We also saw a number of police stationed around us.

Tony nudged me, "Do you notice something unusual?"

I did. The police seemed to be allowing only certain people through their lines. Most were young men, solidly built. Suddenly, the men lunged forward and began to yank the crosses from our necks and tear them in pieces.

The other people standing behind the police lines watched silently as the agitators mocked and shoved us. One of them

climbed up on one of our vans and stuck on a big sign proclaiming: COMMUNISM, NOT CHRIST.

Alan raised his camera to take a picture. A powerfully built, sweater-clad man wrenched it from his hands, opened the back, and pulled out the shiny ribbon of film, exposing it to the light.

There was now only one safe place for our group to be. The other leaders and I called out, "Will the tour group please get inside the hotel!"

Finally, we made it to the sanctuary of the lobby from where we could still hear yells and threats from the outside.

"Wow!" said Alan, "I'm glad they didn't bring *that* bunch to the roadblock."

It was a nervous group of young people that sat down to dinner in the hotel dining room that evening. Moreover, we noticed that Viktor wasn't with us. But a few minutes after we started to eat, we looked up to see him enter the room and head directly for Ted's table. His face was white. He pointed at Ted. "You will have to come with me," he said, his voice trembling. "The chief of police has something important to discuss with you."

Whatever good feelings we may have had as we entered Novgorod that evening, now evaporated. First, the organized attack. And now this!

Would we *ever* get out of Russia?

15

But They Didn't Like Us in Novgorod

It was very quiet in the dining room while Ted was with the chief of police. All that could be heard was the tinkling of silver and glasses as we silently ate.

Then Ted returned and a mass gasp of relief exuded through the room. He shared with us what had happened. He had been escorted down the hall to a little room in which a tall spare man in uniform was introduced to him as chief of police.

They sat down and the chief looked at Ted silently for a moment. Then he told him in no uncertain terms that it was "against Soviet law" for our group to hold religious meetings "anywhere," and that it was illegal to pass out religious literature as we had been doing.

"But I have read Soviet law," stated Ted, "and it states there *is* freedom of religion."

The chief stared impassively at Ted for a moment, then said, "Not the kind of freedom you have in the West."

"Thank you, sir," said Ted. "I appreciate your letting us know. Now we know for certain that your law does not allow religious liberty. You have made it very plain."

Ted drew himself up. "All I can say is that your government's talk of religious liberty is a farce in the light of what you now tell me. People here do not have the liberty to worship God as their conscience dictates."

The chief stared back at Ted. "All I can tell you is that if you continue these things, severe measures will be taken against you and your group."

As Ted continued telling us what happened, we sat quietly at our tables, the food pushed away from us and getting cold. We no longer felt like eating.

Ted echoed our thoughts when he added, "Now we know for sure for we have seen it in practice. Soviet law does not allow for religious freedom of any kind." Then, his face visibly brightening, Ted continued in an optimistic tone of voice, "Brothers and sisters, I think God *has* given us a great victory anyway in what we have accomplished. What has happened today, even the agitators planted outside, has shown us that we can't pigeonhole God. We must realize that each day God has something new for us, and we must continue to remain in a place of prayer where we are sensitive to His guidance and thus know in our hearts what He wants us to do."

As Ted's words sank into our hearts, I looked around the room to see fifty-one people who only two weeks ago were complete strangers. Now, in the words that Ted used, we *were* brothers and sisters as are all Christians who are one in the Spirit.

Tonight would be our last night in Russia. As I looked at faces I had come to know and love, a poignancy filled my heart.

Was it something like this, I wondered, at the Last Supper?

Ted stopped talking for a moment, looking at Viktor and Nadjina, then turned back to us, "Do you love your guides?"

All responded with a "Yes!" that shook the room. Viktor and Nadjina stared at their plates in embarrassment.

"Then," said Ted, seriously, "don't show it."

The room became so still I could sense my heart beat.

"We don't want to put our guides in any situation," continued Ted, "where they will be hurt after we leave."

We all knew what he meant.

"And now," continued Ted, "we'd like to express our appreciation to them. Viktor and Nadjina, would you come up here?"

And this is when we saw how God led James, the former monk, to bring two gifts so particularly appropriate when James had absolutely no idea of who they'd be given to.

Ted presented the young Indian maiden print to Nadjina, and the Indian brave to Viktor "with love from all of us."

"Perhaps they are not of great material value," said Ted, "but we want you to know that they express our deepest appreciation for your help—and patience," he added with a grin.

"In fact," he continued, "you'll find it expressed on the back." Nadjina and Viktor turned their prints over. Each of us had signed the prints and added a little message such as "We love you," "We're praying for you," and Scripture verses.

For a long time the two of them stood there, reading.

"Speech! Speech!" we called out.

Both of them blushed, but you could tell they were deeply pleased. Finally, Viktor spoke. "Well," he smiled, "I really don't know what to say. You have really touched me." Then he grinned, "All I can think of is that some time in the future . . . when you all are not so busy . . ."

We howled with laughter.

". . . I would like you to come back," he continued. "I would like to show you some of Russia . . . like my hometown . . . which," and he smiled broadly, "is Moscow."

Everyone roared and applauded.

Nadjina, embarrassed, stood up with a nervous laugh. Her warm feelings showed through. "I will ditto everything Viktor has already said," she said, "except for one thing. And that is I would like to really show you the most beautiful town in all of Russia—my hometown of Leningrad!"

We then all filed past Viktor and Nadjina to shake hands and personally thank them. We felt this would be our last opportunity to do this. True, we knew they would be with us tomorrow. But for some strange reason, we felt that never again would we enjoy this closeness.

Then Ted said to us, "I don't believe the Lord wants us to do any witnessing outside the hotel tonight." We all knew what he meant. "Let's stay inside and speak for Him here."

Some of the fellows, still stinging from the confrontation outside, wanted to go back out. But Ted said that he had strong guidance not to get involved. "We have completed our mission," he said, "and now we should leave in peace."

Together we prayed about which direction to take and it seemed right that we stay inside. The animosity outside the hotel seemed to be reflected by Lenin, who stared intently at us from a giant portrait suspended in the lobby as we walked out of the dining room.

Soon, spontaneously, we started singing. But then we worried about getting too loud. We started to leave, but the woman in charge of the floor came over. "No, no," she indicated, "please stay here." She ushered us to another part of the lounge. We began singing in the Spirit and many people gathered to listen.

During this time, one of the men who guided us on our last trip through Novgorod approached several of us individually. He acted quite confidential as he asked each person if they had a Bible to give him. We had to tell him we were sorry, that we had none to give. Later, all of us shared the same feeling that he was a plant by the local police. If we had given him a Bible, it could have been cause for us being ejected immediately, that night.

There were others that were not acting suspiciously, such as the group of Russian athletes staying in the hotel. They were going to participate in some local games the next day. They drifted over to hear our singing. And some of our kids spent up to an hour telling of Jesus' love for them. They seemed very responsive.

Finally, we all drifted off to bed for what would be our last night in Russia.

The next morning we went into the dining room for breakfast and found Viktor waiting for us. Accompanying him were two men. Viktor introduced one as the chief of the Intourist Bureau of Novgorod. Ted nudged me and nodded toward the other man. "It's the chief of police," he whispered.

"I have been in contact with Moscow Intourist," said the official, "and they have sent a message that you all are to be expelled from the country immediately."

The reason?

"You have been very poor tourists and have conducted yourselves in an unseemly manner. Not only that, but you have broken Soviet law. You are to be conducted to the border today by special police escort."

If we did not cooperate, he continued, there would be "severe consequences." We were absolutely forbidden to display crosses, call out greetings, or distribute tracts.

"What law have we broken?" asked Ted.

The official replied that there was nothing more to say, turned on his heel, and, along with the police chief, strode out of the room.

Everyone sat there, suddenly feeling the leaden oppression of Soviet officialdom.

We had a hurried breakfast, then quickly got our bags together and went down to the small courtyard in which the vans were parked. The courtyard, we discovered, was not the quiet secluded spot in which we'd left the vans yesterday. It was now jammed with policemen, plainclothesmen, and police cars.

Our team got into our van which had a banner inside the windows: WHY PERSECUTE RUSSIAN CHRISTIANS? Some of the other vans had similar banners.

I climbed in behind the wheel; Nadjina sat next to me. As we waited for Ted to signal us to start, a KGB man charged up to the van ahead of us, his trench coat flying and face flushed with anger. He tore open the door on which Miriam inside had evidently been leaning for she almost flew out with the door. The stocky KGB man lunged inside, ripped out the sign, and slammed the door hard in Miriam's face.

Word flashed among us: "Lock the doors!"

He saw our banner and strode toward us. He pulled at our locked door. His face became purple. "Open! Open!" he shouted, pointing to the lock.

I looked straight ahead, shaking with fear. His fist began to pound at the side of our van like a steel wrecking ball. His anger flaring, he began forcing the door with his knee. I thought about the $75 charge for damages but still ignored him.

Nadjina turned to me. "Don't be ridiculous. This is silly. Open the door!"

By now some of the girls in our bus were crying.

But as I sat there, a powerful sense of the protection of God came over me. It seemed as if time stood still for a moment. I turned to Nadjina. "Nadjina, it isn't silly, it is tragic to know that my brothers and sisters in Christ are being killed and persecuted for their faith in Jesus.

"You know very well that the Christians in this country are among the best workers you have," I continued. "They're conscientious. And they're not interested in political power. All they ask is that they be allowed to worship God in freedom as the Scriptures say. And they are being denied that right.

"Nadjina, it isn't silly, it's tragic."

She turned and remained silent.

The KGB man had left, but suddenly he was at our back door. I had forgotten to lock it. It flew open, he reached in and triumphantly ripped out our sign.

Ted gave the signal to move. As I began shifting gears, an extemperaneous prayer came from my lips: "Lord, bless your chil-

dren who don't have the freedom to worship as we do." I could hear others in the van praying and groaning in the Spirit.

As our caravan slowly pulled out of the courtyard, I discovered I was last in line with a police squad right behind me. One police car? The more we looked the more we saw. Finally we counted fourteen yellow police cars surrounding us like a pack of hounds.

It was gloomy and overcast as we moved out into the barren country. Everything seemed bleak—the mud fields, the potholed roads. All of our exterior crosses had been ripped off but a few still bravely hung inside our windows. No one said much, and most continued to quietly pray. One of the kids pulled another sign saying WHY PERSECUTE SOVIET CHRISTIANS? out from its hiding place under a seat and taped it at the window. Since it faced the side of the road, no police car could see it.

As we drove through towns, we waved, and I'm sure passersby saw our crosses. But we didn't toss out tracts. When we'd stop at a gas station to refuel, the fourteen squad cars would encircle us.

Later, one of our group described the scene and his reaction. "All of us had gotten out to stretch our legs. I glanced around and saw what must have been about thirty policemen standing around guarding us. What have we done to warrant all this? I wondered. And then I realized that they really were afraid of the Word of God. And it came to me that there is nothing in the world that will stem the tide of communism but the Gospel of Jesus Christ. The demons of materialism quake before Him."

The police came up and ordered us to remove the crosses from inside our window. I said I had no authority to do so. "Let me see your driver's license," he demanded. Unwittingly, I showed it to him. He grabbed it from my hand. "I will keep it," he said, "until you get to the border."

Ted came walking up. "Give me your license," ordered the policeman. Ted drew up all his five feet, seven inches, and said, "You're going to have to bodily rough me up to get it."

Ted kept his license.

But the police were emphatic. If we didn't remove every cross, every sign inside and outside, they would confiscate our vans, put us in Intourist buses, and ship us out with nothing but the clothes on our backs.

We decided it was time to stop openly witnessing. We all felt sure that we had done what the Lord wanted us to do. We were now so close to the border. Besides, we had a deadline to meet in London to get the vans back.

Soon we discovered what prompted the "get tough" policy. Leningrad lay just ahead and they didn't want us to go through it as Christians. As we continued on into the city, we found ourselves winding our way around it through its outskirts. With sirens screaming, the police led us through the streets at breakneck speed. Obviously, they were still afraid of what we might do.

Well, if we couldn't witness to those on the outside, then we'd witness to those with us. We had learned that when Nadjina had traveled with Tony's group yesterday, they had talked to her frankly about Jesus. "The Spirit of the Lord was heavy on us," said Tony. "However, Nadjina seemed to laugh at us, until suddenly she became very quiet."

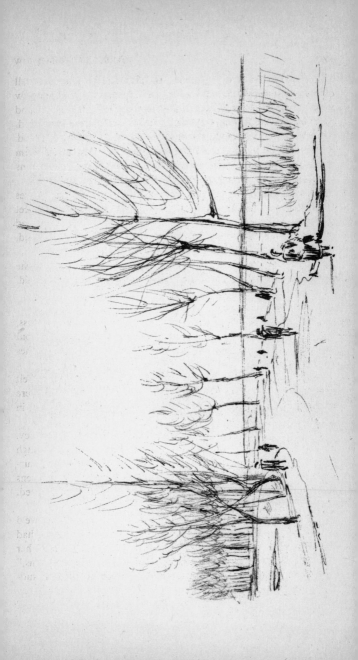

" 'I know I am a sinner,' she blurted, then turned to the window and said nothing for a long time. I have never seen anyone under so heavy a conviction," added Tony.

In our van Nadjina was eager to point out interest spots of her hometown, even though we were far from the beautiful central area. She called our attention to the many new apartment buildings. The rents were very inexpensive, she said, adding that most of these buildings were prefabricated. "One goes up in ninety days," she said proudly.

Suddenly, she was quiet for a moment, then said, "Do you see that building on the horizon?"

We would have missed it but for her pointing it out. In the haze of Leningrad's skyline we could make out a dome with a cross on top of it. "That is a seminary," said Nadjina. "It is where Russian Orthodox priests are trained for the ministry."

One comment and that was all. But we all thought it very significant for Nadjina to point this out. Never, up until now, had she mentioned anything of a religious nature to us.

Perhaps it was knowing we were so close to freedom, perhaps the Lord wanted us to sing for Nadjina's sake. But suddenly, everyone in our van broke out into song. We started to sing Sunday-school choruses like the "Gospel Express," "Climb Up Sunshine Mountain," and "Zacchaeus in the Tree."

Then we started: "He's got the whole world in His hands . . . in His hands." Soon it became: "He's got the KGB in His hands, in His hands."

"What about the FBI?" laughed Nadjina.

We continued: "He's got the FBI in His hands . . ." And then we added: "He's got the CIA in His hands, in His hands . . ."

Nadjina broke out in laughter. I believe this was the greatest witnessing we could have done for Nadjina at this moment. Instead of talking seriously to her, we expressed our love and joy through singing. Soon, she was talking freely.

We asked if she had seen much publicity about the Jesus Movement in the West. "Yes," she said, "I've read about it."

As the kilometers clicked off, we suddenly realized we were approaching the border. Now we began to worry about our films.

"Do you think customs will take our films, Nadjina?"

"Well . . . ," obviously she didn't want to say yes.

We saw the buildings of Vyborg in the distance as we sped on to the border, all fourteen police cars still escorting us. Now, the highway checkpoint scrutiny intensified to where they carefully checked one van through at a time.

"Oh, my," said Gwendolyn, "do they think *anyone* would want to stay *behind?*"

Now we began seeing places that brought back memories. The little turn-off where we had stopped for lunch and kicked the soccer ball around until the Russian army jeep came by.

Had *that* been only four days ago?

Now it was 6 P.M. and the afternoon sun was low over the trees. And then, yes, there it was. Rising above the trees was the custom house tower! '

"Like the gates of heaven," said Rudy softly.

We slowed as we turned into the driveway, almost as if in a dream. As I started to get out, one of the blue-overalled guards started shoving me back. "What's the matter?" I called in irritation. Greg finally was able to decipher the message. "He wants you to get back inside. In fact, they want *everybody* to stay inside."

And so we learned. Leaving Russia was even more complicated than entering. They would check only one van through at a time. Meanwhile, the rest of us had to wait in our vehicles.

By the time they cleared the first van, an hour went by. It was 7 P.M. We hadn't had anything to eat.

Jim's van now moved up. There were two of us left. Now it was after 8 P.M. Another hour went by and, finally, we were waved forward.

As we were stepping out of the van, Nadjina, who had gotten out some time ago, came walking by. "Good-bye, kids!" she said, waving very casually. Suddenly, her eyes filled with tears, she turned her head, and walked away as someone shouted, "We'll be praying for you!"

"That's good," she answered, her face red. She walked from van to van, waving good-bye.

Viktor never did come by. We sensed he felt it was healthier not to.

For the brief time our guides had traveled with us, we felt they had tasted real freedom. When we left, so would their freedom.

I stayed with the van, driving it over to the grease pits where again a careful search of it was made.

Meanwhile, they were going through everybody's luggage. Whenever a roll of film was found, the guard would unroll it and expose it to the light. My slides were still in my camera. Earlier I had worried how it could be hidden. Finally, I decided that I was just going to trust in the Lord and leave it in my bag.

I stepped up to the guard, unzipped my bag, and presented it to him, silently praying. He opened it, saw a lot of dirty laundry. His hand explored inside the bag. The camera was there under the clothes. But somehow he never found it. He zipped the bag closed and handed it back to me.

In the meantime, there was quite a worship service going on at Jim's van. He and the other fellows were praying loudly and singing in the Spirit while the van was being searched. Later Jim said, "We just claimed the blood of Jesus on the van, on all the seats, and the searchers didn't find a thing." When they got to his luggage, they found his camera and opened it. "Where is your film?" they asked. "You should know they don't sell film in your country," Jim answered, which is true.

All the while his film was in a seam of the trench coat he was wearing. They took Jim into a back room and started searching him. "Where's your film?" they demanded.

"I'm not going to give it to you."

"We'll give you one hour," said the guards.

"You're bluffing," said Jim who then walked out to his van. No one stopped him.

About this time, I had headed for the men's room when the big KGB man who had taken my license, stopped me. "Oh, oh," I wondered, "what now?" He handed me back my license. *"Spasibo,* thank you," I said.

Finally, each of our five vans had been checked carefully from inside the gas tank to under the horn ring. We all got in vans, still in a state of suspended animation. We were still not out of Russia, we kept reminding ourselves. Anything could happen.

We drove very gingerly for the next half mile through the dark pines which had an oppressive quality about them. And then we saw it again, the little pine tree growing in the shape of a cross, as if God was reminding us, "I am the beginning and the end."

On we drove, past the deadly open area with the menacing gun towers looming above the trees. And then, there in the late evening light was the red flag with the hammer and sickle, waving above the trees. Beyond it lay freedom!

We rolled on to the red-and-white-striped pike. Now it looked beautiful! The same young soldiers who had checked us in now stepped out to meet us. Quietly, efficiently, they solemnly went over each passport. We wondered if they knew how much had happened since they had last seen us. We sat there afraid to speak, afraid to move. Finally, they handed us back our passports and saluted.

The pike lifted, a silent cheer arose from five vans, and we started up. As we began to move on, we said: *"Spasibo,* thank you, *Christos voskresen!* Christ Is Risen! Jesus loves you!" It was the last time we were to say that in Russia.

The red-and-white-striped pike now pointed like a finger to heaven. We rolled past it into Finland.

All of us were praising Him, and singing as we moved on to the Finnish border. Just one guard was there to meet us at the border house. He came out with a big smile, collected our passports, stamped each of them quickly, and handed them back wishing us, "Godspeed!" I started in surprise. It was the first time in seven days we heard someone not from our group use His name in blessing.

We drove slowly on, everyone anticipating what was coming.

Soon, Ted signaled and our caravan pulled over to the side of the forested road. Like an explosion, every door flew open and all fifty-one of us tumbled out. We leaped up and down on the highway, hugged each other, praised the Lord, and began singing: "Hallelujah, For the Lord Our God the Almighty Reigns."

We had made it. We were free at last.

But we still had a long way to go.

16

Going Home Is Half the Fun

We could have danced and leaped all night as we celebrated our freedom in the middle of that Finnish highway. Finally, Ted raised his hand. "The Finnish border guard gave me a note," he announced. It was for William Mather, a Christian journalist, who was traveling with us.

Ted began to read it: "Praise God for your great victories." It was from one of Mr. Mather's fellow Christian journalists who had traveled separately from our group.

We all looked at each other for a moment. The truth was beginning to dawn on us. Yes, it *was* a victory. This was the first time we had heard anyone else claim it as such. It was a boost we needed. Mr. Mather went on to say his group had called the story in to United Press International wire service. They were also arranging television and press conferences for us in London.

We began to feel like celebrities.

"Okay, let's not let it go to our heads," called Ted, "we've still a long way to go."

We climbed back into the minibuses and started the long trip home. Home! To a few of the kids it was right here in Finland. To others it was England. To me, it was 6,000 miles away. As we rolled along through the corridor of tall pines in the darkening twilight, I thought how beautiful Finland looked. And then I remembered how cold and drab it seemed to be only a few days ago as we headed toward Russia. Then we had fear in our hearts.

The trees thinned as a little town came into view and there was an American-style gas station! *Mobil* glowed in colors above the brightly lit station. How good it was to see advertising again. How we missed it, the color of the free world, color in stores, color on the streets. As one of our group said, there seemed to be no color in Russia, everything looked so drab. "Even the new buildings all looked twenty years old," he said.

Finally we pulled up to our contact house in Helsinki. A steaming supper was waiting, but we were starved for something different. Everyone rushed to find their Bibles. When one is used to living with a Bible in pocket or purse, to be denied it for even a few days is spiritual starvation. Soon, all over the house you could see kids sitting on the floor or draped over chairs reading their Bibles like hungry people eating steak and potatoes.

I thought of Matthew 4:4—"man shall not live by bread alone, but by every word that proceeds from the mouth of God."

Then Alan sprang up, lifting his Bible. "Here it is!" he exclaimed. "This is our confirmation."

As Alan read Psalms 124, it was as if the Lord was speaking directly to us through him:

> If it had not been the Lord who was on our side, let Israel now say . . . When men rose up against us, then they would have swallowed us up alive, when their anger was kindled against us . . . Blessed be the Lord who has not given us as prey to their teeth! We have escaped as a bird from the snare of the fowlers; the snare is broken and we have escaped!

The psalm told our whole story.

Not until we were surfeited with His Word did the kids think about eating. Then, even though the hour was late, we decided to press on. Like homing pigeons we couldn't travel fast enough. We headed out hoping to catch the 1 A.M. ferry that would take us back across the Baltic. We missed it—the first one we missed on this trip. But now it didn't matter. The important part of our journey was behind us.

We tried to sleep in the minibuses at the dock. Somehow I

couldn't get my long legs adjusted to the cramped quarters. I got up and went to the men's room. I was feeling very grimy and travel worn. I got a towel, wet it, and rubbed it over my stubble. I was getting sick of my condition and my clothes. I wanted to get home as soon as possible.

Friday, May 4th, dawned bright and clear with a brisk breeze chopping the waters of the harbor. We boarded the 10 A.M. ferry and bought breakfast on ship. As I paid for my glass of milk and Danish roll, I realized it was the first money I had spent since before entering Russia. When one leaves the U.S.S.R., he can't take any Russian money with him. So I had to show the border officials my slip which stated the amount of money I had when I came in: two rubles, twenty kopeks. And that's the exact amount I still had. The official was surprised. I didn't tell him I was so busy I didn't have a chance to buy anything.

The ship was peaceful and quiet as we steamed along the sparkling Baltic. It was unlike the rousting night on which we last traveled on her. But that was a Friday night and this was Friday morning. About halfway across the sea, we stopped at an island to leave off a merry bunch of high-school students on an outing. I couldn't help comparing them to the Russian teen-agers we saw who, for the most part, seemed so serious and quiet compared to these happy youths who streamed off the ship swinging their knapsacks, laughing and singing.

Soon the Swedish port of Norrtalje could be seen on the horizon and all of us stood at the rail silently watching. Everyone's thoughts were on home.

The ship pulled into the Swedish port and as we disembarked, there was a rumor that Ted was trying to get us into a youth hostel in Stockholm. Our hearts jumped in joy since we hadn't been looking forward to crawling into those damp tents. Most of us still had our colds.

We rolled into Stockholm in the early evening. And again we marveled at the beauty of this city. At one point our road wound along a river and we gasped at a lovely old gothic church steeple outlined against the glowing western sky. We crossed bridge after bridge and finally pulled up to two old ships moored in the harbor. This was our youth hostel and, though unusual, it promised to be dry and warm. We stowed our gear in the little cabins and then went out searching for a telephone. I wanted to talk to Rozanne more than anything else.

Finally we found a place where one could phone and send telegrams. I settled in a soundproof booth and put through my collect call. It seemed an interminable time. Then, I heard the phone ringing six thousand miles away in Morristown, New Jersey, where Rozanne was staying with her parents.

Someone lifted the receiver. "Hello?" It was Rozanne!

"Hello, Honey," I shouted, "I love you!"

Rozanne's voice was so beautiful, so warm. Suddenly I was intensely homesick. I wanted to leap into the harbor outside and start swimming madly west.

We talked long, saying all the things husbands and wives think of after long separations. Then, I was given the momentous news. Anita had started walking! Yes, she had taken her first steps. I

tried to figure out where I had been when she had made this great advance. About the closest I could figure was that Anita had taken her first step as our group stepped across the Russian border.

The next morning we stopped in the United States Embassy in Stockholm to inform them of our Russian visit and standing in the reception area was the American flag. Somehow seeing this familiar old symbol so far from home was like finding a dear friend. Suddenly, I walked over and kissed it. I looked around, feeling self-conscious; the man at the desk was watching me with a smile. "Don't feel bashful," he laughed.

Back into the vans we climbed to continue our race home. On to Copenhagen, and into Hanover, Germany, we drove, retracing our route back to England.

There wasn't as much talking as there was on the trip to Russia. Somehow, it seemed everyone had something to think about, and there was much quiet contemplation out the window. The only one talking now, in fact, was Greg, who was deep in conversation with Sheena. I smiled to myself; it was wonderful how

Greg had emerged from his shell, and it was all because others had taken an interest in him—*made* him talk, actually.

Too often, I thought, does the aggressively social person become the leader while the quiet, introspective one is left behind. In a Christ-centered group, the wallflower is loved into bloom.

As we continued on, our group began to break apart. In Germany, Tony, Jim, Greg, and Chris took off in different directions, some to catch planes for home, others to continue Christian evangelism training and mission work. It was difficult saying good-bye. By now we had become a family.

As we drove on, we looked forward to a new excitement. Ted told us that Brother Andrew planned to meet us at our campsite in Holland. The anticipation at meeting Brother Andrew took the sting out of having to climb into the soggy tents again, and we drove on with enthusiasm. As we rolled through the land of canals and windmills, we were impressed by the cleanliness and pride peope took in their lawns and the profusion of flowers they grew. Of course, we also realized that things had done a lot of greening since we'd been through this part of Europe last.

Finally we reached the campground and set up our tents. Ted made a call and in about thirty minutes Brother Andrew drove up.

I stood in awe as we waited for him to get out of the car. I had read his book *God's Smuggler* and marveled at his adventures, how he single-handedly smuggled carloads of Bibles past Iron Curtain guards. I remembered how sometimes the Bibles would be accidently laying right out in the open in his car. Brother Andrew would silently pray and it was as if the inspecting guard's eyes were blinded when he came to the Bibles.

Perhaps it was because of my hero worship but I was expecting a giant to step out of that car. Instead, I was surprised to see a very average-looking man of medium build and height. And then I realized how God works. Brother Andrew was the kind of man who could slip by in a crowd unnoticed anywhere, the man who again and again could pass through border customs without arousing recognition or suspicion. He was the man best suited to do this kind of work.

No, Brother Andrew's strength was not in the physical. But

when you looked into his eyes you could see the power there, the deep spiritual strength that knew no fear or intimidation. I felt it was the Spirit of God and was honored to shake his hand.

Brother Andrew filled us in on what happened to the other group that flew direct to Moscow. It turned out that most of them were confined to their hotels on May Day.

"The Russians told them that they had heard that a group of Christian radicals were coming to stage a demonstration and they couldn't allow anyone out of their hotel," said Brother Andrew.

We all laughed. We were the "radicals."

Sixteen youths did get out of their hotel, he said, and witnessed in a park—they were promptly arrested and expelled.

"It was obvious the Russian government had gotten wind of your trip and were scared," said Brother Andrew. He explained that the Gospels of John which had been smuggled into Russia for us to distribute on May Day were in good hands. "The Russian Christians will hand them out instead," he said, "and this too, will be very effective."

Summing it up, he continued, "I feel the Russian Christians were greatly encouraged by your outreach. Not everybody was for it. Many in the official church were scared, but those in the underground church were enthusiastic."

As Brother Andrew talked, it became even more obvious to us that we really had a victory. And now I could see how well God worked things out. If we had reached Moscow, our demonstration would have been quickly squashed. However, God had chosen the time and place: the roadblock. It was a time least expected by the authorities, and a place where we were able to witness to the utmost. We thought of the thousands of Russians who would not have heard our message in any other way; the police and military men at the roadblock, the buses and cars full of people that passed by, the hotels in which we stayed, and all the people in Kalinin, Novgorod, and the many towns and cities our Jesus caravan passed through.

We bowed our heads with Brother Andrew as he prayed for us and gave thanks for God's victory.

The next day we drove straight through, from Belgium to

France and then via hovercraft to England where late that night found our tired little caravan winding its way down the dark cobblestone street to finally slump at the curb in front of the vicarage. Our journey was over.

I remember Sheri meeting Ted at the door, the light brightening her face as she opened it and the two falling into each other's arms.

The next day we returned the vans to the much-relieved owner and I made my plane reservations for New York. Later, some of us were interviewed on a television program. The man who did the questioning kept asking why we wanted to go to Russia and bother people who "obviously wished to remain atheist."

"You could have caused an international incident," he snapped.

We wondered where *his* sympathy lay, but the kids answered him beautifully, remembering that a soft answer turneth away wrath. The Lord seemed to give them not only wisdom in their replies which deflated every criticism, but their love shone through for this man who was obviously trying to get them angry.

It was another victory, the first of many adventures that would keep on happening we found, even though our journey was over.

Later, we had our final sharing session together. Ted told us of his burden for continuing to work for Christians in Communist lands. "It's something I feel He wants me to do," said Ted, "and Sheri says she's with me all the way."

Others gave their testimonies. Many revealed that the Lord had been speaking to them about learning the Russian language. And fifteen said that they would continue to work in this ministry to Christians in other suppressed countries such as Hungary, East Germany, and Czechoslovakia. In seeking the Lord's guidance on this, they had already been led to a decision to study Eastern European languages.

Our little group stayed up late as we continued to share. No one wanted to go to bed, not wanting to miss any of this, our last night together.

It was very difficult the next morning as we said our goodbyes. For we all had truly become like brothers and sisters. Perhaps we would never see each other again. None of us knew where the Lord would lead us.

But as we embraced and looked at each other through unashamed tears, we knew in our hearts that we would always be bonded together in the memories of the adventure we shared.

I waved one last good-bye, turned, and stepped down the old stone steps of the vicarage. I stood for a moment on the old cobblestone street which I had walked up so hesitantly three weeks ago. The same mist was falling on the black iron fence. But as I looked up at the old vicarage, it did not look so foreboding anymore. It was like leaving an old friend.

I knew that I had changed inside. No longer was I a somewhat hesitant Christian, still fearful of the future, conserving myself to face material responsibilities.

In taking this trip I had placed complete trust in the Lord, for I had taken it for only one reason—I had been led.

I had hung all my faith on His guidance, and it had held.

I hoisted my duffel bag to my shoulder, turned, and looked ahead, confident that from now on wherever He would lead me, I would be able to take that step gladly and quickly.

As I sat in the plane to New York, I looked back on my life and saw how God had led me through it in steps, teaching me something new in each one. My pastorates and Teen Challenge work were each a time of enlightenment. Now I sensed I was again changing gears to step into a new kind of outreach ministry.

Before I realized it, my plane was making its approach to Kennedy Airport. After disembarking, I momentarily hesitated as I approached customs, then relaxed—this was the United States. Soon I was at the passenger gates. There was Dad and Mother—but no Rozanne or Anita!

Dad pointed down the hall. Anita had been fussing and Rozanne had taken her to a bench to calm her since they were not sure exactly when my plane would be in. I raced down the hall. Rozanne stood up holding Anita, her face radiant.

We were in each other's arms, the three of us. I was home again.

Epilogue

Many months have passed since that 1973 May Day when fifty-one of us stood on that rainy highway seventy miles this side of Moscow—many months in which our thinking has seasoned about our joyful invasion.

Was it really a victory?

Yes, in many ways.

That fifty-one young people risked their freedom to go to Russia and openly witness for Christ on behalf of their Russian brothers and sisters certainly gave great encouragement to suppressed Christians everywhere.

It contradicted reports that the western world had become so materialistic that it had forgotten Russian believers and their suffering. It also helped belie the story told to Russian young people that western youth are not religious and, instead, are all becoming revolutionists and leftists.

Not only did we encourage young Russian Christians but challenged Communist youth's atheistic instruction that religion is the opiate of the masses when they saw happy, courageous young people risking their freedom for Christ.

In short, they saw that the Christian witness surpasses the so-called sacrificial spirit of communism in that communism sacrifices only for itself, but Christians sacrifice for others.

As I write this, there is much news about the "détente" achieved between our country and the Soviet Union, the relaxing of international tensions. This is all well and good. But the paradox in news reports from Russia continues. On one hand, Russia has made a surface show of softening its iron-handed treatment of religious groups, both Christian and Jew. Yet, on the other hand, both regular news and underground sources report intensified police-state oppression of its own subjects.

In our country we are blessed with an abundance of religious freedom. We take so much for granted while our brothers and sisters behind the Iron Curtain eagerly search for crumbs. We who live free reject more of Christianity in an hour than they are able to get their hands on in five years. My brief view of their suffering has given me a burden for them. I owe them much. I cannot worship freely here and not think about the Christians of Russia.

It is a country where believers are persecuted because they have the courage to stand up and give the bread of life to the starving millions. It is a country where our guides were not even sure that a Bible could be purchased. They claimed there was a paper shortage. Yet, in Vyborg they were giving away *free* books on Lenin and Marx and other propaganda written in English.

I realize that I am now probably blacklisted by the Russian government and may never be able to enter that country again. If so, I pray that the Lord will wipe it off the books so that I can return. If not, I will continue to do what I can to spread the vision to other young people.

I feel that American young people with their new vision of Christ, their exuberant courage, and spirit of sacrifice are being called to continue this joyful invasion in taking His message of love and hope to these suppressed people. But the message of Christ must be taken in love. There is no place for vengeance or hate in this ministry. There is also one thing *all of us* can do, and that is to pray daily for the people of Russia.

I know that I will pray every day that we in the United States will help provide spiritual strength and comfort with our prayers, our sacrifice, and our personal presence among the Russian people, a beautiful, warm, and friendly people, but a sad, quietly desperate people isolated from God and starving for His love.

Christ has shown us the way—we must feed His sheep.

EPILOGUE TO THE SECOND EDITION

During the 20th century, more Christians have died for their faith than in all the other 19 preceding centuries.

Almost one year to the day after my return from the Soviet Union, I attended a news conference in New York City where a Russian Baptist evangelist spoke about human rights for Christians in the Soviet Union. He was a close friend and associate of the famous Baptist leader Georgi Vins. Under special arrangement between West Germany and the Soviet Union, he had been allowed to emigrate to West Germany.

After his speech, I approached him to share about our missionary trip to his country one year earlier. As I began to explain, his eyes lighted up and he said he knew all about it. "In fact," he explained, "the news of your coming spread throughout the church in the Soviet Union and caused much joy and encouragement!"

To me it was another confirmation of God's purpose for this trip.

When our fifty-one young people entered the Soviet Union that April morning, it was like one of the first waves of Marines that landed on Guadacanal during World War II. They established a beachhead. Reinforcements then followed to claim the land.

Our goal was to establish that kind of beachhead in the minds of Christians everywhere, to prove that much more can be done for Christ in a communist country than ever imagined. And we were not the only ones. Many similar groups of young Christians were already at work in communist countries, as they are today, sharing Christ with the people and providing Bibles and literature. Normally, these groups do not make headlines since their work is best achieved quietly without fanfare.

All of this shows that Christians can do much more than ever believed in a communist country. Misgivings and preconceived notions or impossible odds against witnessing turn out to be illusions undoubtedly propagated by the Enemy himself. There is no excuse why we cannot follow Jesus Christ's Great Commission and evangelize *all* the world. There is no such thing as pockets where we cannot enter!

Our little adventure proves that when God gives Christians a vision for a communist country, they can step out in faith fully expecting God to use them in communicating His message despite the "roadblocks" the enemy throws up.

Paul, the Apostle, said in Philippians 1:12, 14: "Now I want you to know, brethren, that my circumstances have turned out for the greater progress of the Gospel. And that most of the brethren, trusting in the Lord because of my imprisonment, have far more encouragement to speak the Word of God without fear."

As I meditated on these words, I thought about our group's own imprisonment through house arrest and how the story resulting from it has encouraged many to greater boldness in working for the Lord.

Many who read the first edition of *Roadblock to Moscow* wrote to say how God had earlier spoken to them about working for Christ in communist lands, yet they had feared it was impossible. But after reading about our little group, they realized it could be done and wanted more information to prepare for such a ministry.

Thus we have established a resource center called *Truth Invasions* to provide information on the persecuted church and the many opportunities open to all Christians for evangelism in communist countries.

We stand ready to provide information on request and offer our facilities in channeling contributions to ministries and organizations involved in this work. A bimonthly newsletter will be published to provide information on what Christians are accomplishing in communist countries.

Most important, we ask everyone to join us in intercessory prayer for the lonely Christians now suffering tribulation for their faith. We know they are praying for us.

If you wish to participate or share in a continuing ministry of evangelism to communist lands, send your inquiries and gifts to Truth Invasions, Box 117A, R.D. 2, New Ringgold, PA 17960.